Marguerite Patten's
100 Top Teatime Treats

Grub Street • London

Published in 2005 by
Grub Street
4 Rainham Close
London
SW11 6SS
Email: food@grubstreet.co.uk
Web: www.grubstreet.co.uk

Originally published in 1989 as *The Complete Book of Teas* by Piatkus Books

British Library Cataloguing in Publication Data

Patten, Marguerite
Marguerite Patten's 100 top teatime treats
1.Cake 2. Pastry 3. Afternoon teas
I. Title II 100 top teatime treats
641.8'65

ISBN-10 : 1 904943 29 2

Printed and bound in Spain

Contents

Acknowledgements

Marguerite Patten would like to thank the following people
for their helpful information:

The Tea Council Ltd
Dominic Beddard, Wilson Smithett & Co, Tea Brokers
R Twining and Company Ltd
Miss G A Holloway, Chief Home Economist, The Flour Advisory Bureau Ltd
Suranja Cooradia, Novosti Press Agency
The Tea Board of India
D R Collard, The Anglo-Arab Association
Simon Halewood, Promotion and Public Relations Manager, Japan National
Tourist Organization
Chinese Embassy
Moroccan Tourist Office

The Pleasures of Tea

This book has been written in praise of tea, which for many millions of people throughout the world is the drink they enjoy most. Many words have been written and spoken about tea and you will find some of the most noteworthy in the pages that follow. Just why is tea such an enjoyable beverage? Surely it is because it fulfils our various needs: it refreshes us when we are thirsty; warms us when we are cold and yet it can cool us if we are hot; it stimulates us if we are tired and weary, and consoles us if we feel depressed.

Afternoon tea is one of the most pleasing of meals; the food can be cooked or prepared at leisure. It provides an ideal time to relax with family or friends. Visitors to Britain are disappointed if they do not have an opportunity to sample our traditional teatime fare. There are many recipes for afternoon tea and that uniquely British meal – high tea – in this book. They come from various parts of Britain and from other tea-loving and English-speaking countries too.

Tea is a very versatile commodity; it can be served in many different ways. Try some of the hot or cold punches and wine or fruit cups on pages 26 to 41 or the delicious frozen desserts that are given in the same chapter. Different nations serve tea in a variety of ways; the customs of a number of tea-producing and tea-drinking nations will be found in the chapter beginning on page 16.

There is a long and fascinating history associated with *Camellia sinensis*, the tea bush from which the leaves are gathered to produce the tea we find loose in packets or in teabags. It is not easy in these modern days to imagine the hardships endured by the seamen who first brought tea into Britain in their slow-moving sailing ships; we would have been a less fortunate nation if they had not succeeded. The Reverend Smith, who lived during the late eighteenth and into the middle of the nineteenth century and is renowned for the succinctness of his comments on contemporary life, said of tea (and who can disagree?):

'Thank God for Tea
What would the world do without Tea.'

Tea and tea drinking have changed many habits in Britain since tea was first introduced here in 1657; it superseded ale as the usual breakfast drink and took the place of coffee as the favourite beverage. Tea added interest to the famous Pleasure Gardens of the late eighteenth and early nineteenth centuries and they may not have been so successful if tea had not been one of the attractions. Tea played an important role in the development of our pottery industry, which has become world renowned. The beautiful tea-sets produced in the past and today not only grace British tea tables but are exported to the four corners of the world.

Most children learn the words:

'Polly, put the kettle on, we'll all have tea.'

How often are similar words uttered in homes throughout Britain and many other countries of the world as the inhabitants look forward to a welcoming cup of tea?

Marguerite Patten

Cookery Notes

The ingredients for the recipes in this book are given in Imperial, metric and American measures. Tips for following the recipes are given on page 50.

Growing Tea

Tea is the name universally given to the leaves and leaf bud of the evergreen tree or bush, *Camellia sinensis*, also known as Chinese camellia. This flourishes in the warmth of tropical and semi-tropical regions. It likes an acidic soil and needs at least 50 inches/125 cm of rain during the year to encourage the growth of the tender green leaves and leaf buds, known as the 'flush'. The leaves of the tea plant are similar to those of myrtle or privet and are small, oval in shape, dark green and glossy. If the plant is allowed to develop naturally it bears white flowers, not unlike those of a wild rose.

The principal tea-growing areas are China (the first country in which tea was grown and where more varieties of tea are produced than in any other country), India (which now produces 30 per cent of the world's tea and exports to 78 different countries), Sri Lanka (though the teas are still called Ceylon teas), East Africa (chiefly Kenya, Uganda, Rwanda, Burundi, Tanzania, Malawi and Zimbabwe), Mauritius, Papua New Guinea, Japan, Russia, Turkey, Bangladesh, Taiwan, Indonesia, Iran and parts of South America. Some of the teas are sold under the name of the country of origin, others are an important component of tea blends (see pages 21-22).

Preparing the tea estates

Tea bushes are cultivated in plantations, generally known as tea estates, and preparing them is a major task: often the ground must be terraced to prevent erosion of the prepared soil, and it may be necessary to erect windshields to protect the tea bushes from the monsoons which occur in Southeast Asia from the Arabian Sea to China, and in parts of India.

Most tea estates are planted with young bushes grown from cuttings or 'clones'. These are planted out in nursery beds where they stay until they reach 12 inches/30 cm in height, at which stage they are transplanted to their permanent sites. After two years of careful tending the young bushes receive their first pruning. If left unchecked tea plants would grow to a height of 15-30 feet/4.5-9 m, but in cultivation they are pruned to keep them as 3-5 feet/1-1.5 m bushes. This encourages a plentiful growth of leaves, rather than excess wood, and makes picking easier.

Picking

Tea picking, also known as 'plucking', first takes place when the plants are four to five years old. A single bush yields about 4 oz/100 g of leaves and buds in a day. Much picking is done by hand and the majority of pickers are women. An experienced picker can gather 100 pounds/50 kg of leaves and buds in a single day. The normal practice is to remove just the top two leaves and the leaf bud from the flat top of the bush, known as the 'plucking plateau'. This demands skill and dexterity, and care must be taken not to remove any of the stalk.

In low-lying areas there are periods of rapid growth which enable plucking to take place every four days, while in upper areas plucking can only take place at intervals of 12-14 days or more. In each case it is only the new growth that is plucked. In some countries plucking takes place throughout the year, although the season can affect the quality of the tea. In other areas it is confined to specific months.

The leaves are carried in baskets, and when full, the leaves are weighed and the pickers are paid accordingly. The next stage in the production sequence follows quickly, while the leaves are fresh.

Processing

There are various methods of processing, according to the type of tea required. Although there are about 1,500 different types of tea, they all come from the same plant – *Camellia sinensis*. It is the altitude, the type of soil and the weather conditions in the areas in which the plants are grown, and the treatment of the leaves after plucking, which give the individual flavour and character to a particular tea.

The traditional (orthodox) method of processing varies with the type of tea required. The three main types of tea are:

Black or fermented tea. The tea from most countries is processed to become the familiar black dried leaf used throughout the world. The fresh leaves are taken to the factory and spread out on withering troughs. These allow the air to circulate through them and after 8-16 hours, depending on the moisture content of the leaves and the weather conditions, the leaves become limp. The process is known as withering. When the weather is cold and damp, warm air is passed through the leaves to speed up the process.

The leaves are then passed through an orthodox rolling machine which twists them and breaks their veins, releasing natural juices and enzymes. On contact with air these begin to ferment or oxidize. The amount of rolling will vary according to the type of tea required.

The leaves are then spread out on clinically clean tables and left to ferment in a cool but humid atmosphere for three hours, by which time they turn bright orange in colour. The final stage is to dry the leaves until they become black.

Green or unfermented tea. The leaves, which keep their green colour, are steamed, rolled and dried but not fermented. Japan, parts of China, Russia and some Arab countries consume green tea.

Oolong or semi-fermented tea. These teas are treated like green teas, but are partially fermented. Taiwan (formerly Formosa) uses oolong tea.

In recent years changes have been introduced into tea processing. The first development was the use of the CTC (Cut, Tear, Curl) machine, which replaced the orthodox rolling machine. The CTC cuts, tears and curls the tea leaves in a single process and the use of orthodox rollers is partially or completely eliminated, thereby speeding up the process.

Grading and Packing

Once processed, all types of tea must be graded. The terms used reflect the size of the leaf particle, not the quality or flavour of the tea. However, if the word 'flowery' appears, it denotes the fact that the tea contains a high percentage of the leaf buds, which is considered an advantage. Grades of tea leaves:

Larger leaves. Orange Pekoe, Pekoe, Pekoe Souchong. These produce less strong tea, but one with a great deal of flavour and fragrance.

Smaller or broken leaves. Broken Orange Pekoe, Broken Pekoe, Broken Pekoe Souchong. These teas, like the Fannings (below), give stronger tea.

Fannings or small leaves. Pekoe Fannings, Fannings. These teas give more colour to the beverage and a stronger brew.

Dust. This term may sound derogatory but it simply means the smallest leaf particle size, which gives tea a good strength and quick infusion. Smaller leaves are very suitable for modern teabags.

After grading, the tea is securely packed in traditional wooden chests or 'multiwall' paper sacks (sacks made from layers of strong paper) lined with metal foil. These are weighed and stamped before being transported by road, rail or sea to their destination.

Testing and Tasting Tea

When tea arrives at its destination it is checked and weighed and samples are drawn for tasting and evaluation by qualified tea-tasters.

Most people have seen wine-tasters at work and know it is a highly skilled profession. Tea-tasters are equally talented. At a tasting, tea is made from each sample in separate pots and infused according to the taster's requirements. The liquid tea is poured into a bowl. The taster checks the flavour of the tea by sucking the liquid into his or her mouth and allowing it to linger there long enough for the flavour to be appreciated. He then spits it out. The infused leaves and the dry leaves are also inspected. The taster is assessing the flavour, smell, and colour and the uniformity of size of the dry leaves.

Tea Auctions

After the tea is assessed and valued it is put up for auction. A selling broker or auctioneer acts for the estates which grow the tea, while buying brokers act on behalf of the blenders and packers who wish to purchase it. Tea auctions are held in many countries, but the London auction is unique because it deals with teas from all over the world.

Tea Blending

Tea is a natural product and its quality and flavour can vary from week to week. Blenders and packers have to maintain a competitive price, plus consistency of quality and flavour, for their blends, so in order to achieve the desired result teas must be constantly blended. The tea-blender's job, therefore, is highly skilled, and will often involve blending 25 or more different teas. Even some speciality teas are blended.

The final stage is packing the loose tea – or putting it into teabags – then labelling the product so consumers can see at a glance that they are buying their favourite blend and brand.

The History of Tea

The history of tea drinking dates back many centuries and during the years since its inception tea has given pleasure to millions of people throughout the world.

There are two fascinating legends about the origin of the tea bush. One of these tells the story of the Buddhist monk Bodhidharma from India, who travelled to China to preach the message of the Lord Buddha. He fell asleep during his devotions. When he awoke he was overcome with remorse, so he cut off his eyelids and threw them on the ground. The eyelids immediately took root and grew into the evergreen tea bush. The monk plucked some of the leaves from the bush, infused them in boiling water, drank the infusion and instantly felt refreshed.

The second legend is of a Chinese Emperor called Shen Nung, who lived around 2737 BC. He sat under a tree as he boiled water for drinking. A leaf from *Camellia sinensis* fell into the boiling water and gave the Emperor his first cup of tea.

It is recorded that tea bushes grew wild in China some 5,000 years ago and it was there that tea was first produced. Tea is mentioned in a Chinese dictionary dated AD 350 and the *Book of Tea* (*Ch'a Ching*) was written by Lu Yu, a scholar who lived during the Tang dynasty, in about AD 780. This was the first of many Chinese books to be written about tea. Lu Yu covered the choice of tea, the correct method of brewing it, together with ways of serving the beverage and the value of tea as a healthy drink. As far as one can gather, the tea leaves were formed into a kind of cake, steamed, crushed and then moulded. To prepare the drink the cake was toasted, then shredded and steeped in boiling salted water before being served. A tax on tea was imposed during the Tang period.

The cultivation of tea spread fairly rapidly from China to Japan where the first mention of tea in Japanese literature was in AD 593 and a Japanese handbook on tea was written in the thirteenth century. Throughout the ages the drinking of tea and the importance of the ritual tea ceremony has been appreciated in that country (see page 18). Countries bordering China, such as northern India, Burma, Siam (now Thailand) and Indochina, also discovered the pleasures of drinking tea and this was encouraged by Buddhist priests to combat the excessive drinking of alcohol.

The word 'tea' was not used originally. A Chinese local Amoy dialect gives the name as *'t'e'*, pronounced 'tay'. The Cantonese used the word *'ch'a'*, pronounced 'char'. This word was also used in Japan, India and other countries when they first grew tea plants. Nowadays if people in Britain talk about a cup of 'char' it may be regarded as slang, but in fact they are using one of the earliest words for this drink.

Parts of the Arab world learned about tea as early as the middle of the ninth century for they were great seafarers and traders, who obviously discovered it in their travels to the East. The Arab love of the beverage, especially mint tea, continues today (see page 19).

The Dutch, through their active and successful trading companies, first brought tea to Europe in about 1610 – the Venetians, Portuguese and Russians being the first people to enjoy it. It is thought that tea reached England in 1633 (it was first recorded as being sold as a drink there in 1657), Paris in 1648 and America just two years later. Tea would have been enjoyed much later in Australia when settlers, as opposed to convicts, made their homes in that country in the early nineteenth century.

Tea in Britain

The first newspaper advertisement for tea in Britain appeared in 1658: 'That excellent and by all physicians approved, China drink, called by the Chinese "Tcha" and by other nations "Tay", alias "Tee" is sold at the Sultaness Head Cophee [coffee] House in Sweetings Rents by the Royal Exchange, London.'

The popularity of tea in England is partly attributed to Catherine of Braganza (daughter of the future King of Portugal), who came to England in May 1662 to marry Charles II and brought chests of tea with her, for she was a great lover of this beverage.

At this time tea could be purchased in coffee houses as well as in milliners' shops and chemists, and from dealers in silk and chinaware. Towards the latter part of the seventeenth century England consumed more coffee than tea, whereas in America tea had become more popular than coffee. The coffee houses of London were meeting places for social, political and business gatherings, so that paradoxically one can say that the growing awareness of tea was due in no small measure to coffee houses. Charles II claimed that these coffee houses were centres of sedition and they must be closed. This edict caused such bad feeling that he did not enforce the law, so that by the year 1700 there were more than 2,000 coffee houses in London.

Tea was obviously a favourite brew with Dr William Brady, the chaplain to the court of William III and Queen Mary during their reign, which spanned the years 1689 to 1694. He wrote a poem entitled The Tea Table which described tea as 'the sovereign drink of pleasure and health'.

Tea drinking was encouraged in Scotland by Mary of Modena, the beautiful wife of the then Duke of York, who later became James II. He held court at Holyrood House in 1681 in his position of High Commissioner. Tea was served, so giving the official blessing to the drink. At first medical men and clergy in Scotland denounced this new drink but by the middle of the eighteenth century it was firmly established there.

In England the benefits of tea were remarked upon in 1750 when a certain medical treatise on tea was published by Dr Thomas Short as part of his 'Discourse on Tea'. This included these words:

> What should mightily recommend the use of Tea to Gentlemen of a sprightly Genius,
> who would preserve the continuance of their lively and distinct Ideas,
> is its eminent and unequalled Power to take off; or prevent Drowsiness and Dullness, Damps
> and Clouds on the Brain, and intellectual Faculties.
> It begets a watchful Briskness, dispels Heaviness; it keeps Eyes wakeful, the Head clear,
> animates the intellectual Powers, maintains or raises lively Ideas,
> excites and sharpeneth the Thoughts, gives fresh Vigour and Force to Invention,
> awakens the Senses and clears the Mind.

By this time tea was becoming extremely popular among the more wealthy members of the British population, such as the Duke of Wellington who declared that 'tea cleared my head and left me with no misapprehension' and the writer Dr Samuel Johnson who was stated to be 'a hardened and shameless tea drinker, who has for twenty years, diluted his meals with only the infusion of this fascinating plant. Whose kettle has scarcely time to cool. Who with tea amuses the evening, with tea solaces the midnight and with tea welcomes the morning.' Dr Johnson's fondness for tea is confirmed by the historian Macauley, who, when writing about the late Dr Johnson, referred to the fact that he 'swallowed his tea in oceans'.

The price of tea at that time made it available only to the rich and even they were known to use the same tea leaves more than once. A pound of cheapest tea could cost approximately one-third of an average skilled worker's weekly wage.

Tea was highly taxed in Britain in the eighteenth century and two-thirds of the tea drunk was smuggled into the country. In 1784 the Commutation Act cut the tax from 119% to just 12.5%. The lower price meant tea became available to more people, so that by the beginning of the nineteenth century the habit of tea drinking was firmly established; tea had become more popular than coffee, and was accepted as a drink for all classes.

Tea had always been sold loose and this habit provided an ideal opportunity for some unscrupulous grocers to adulterate good tea by mixing it with mouldy or poor-quality tea. There were even reports of 'smouch' being added to black tea – this unpleasant addition was produced from ash trees soaked in copperas (ferrous sulphate) and sheep's dung. The buds of elder trees were blended with green tea.

In 1826 a grocer by the name of John Horniman started selling unadultered good-quality tea in sealed packets of a consistent weight and with a guaranteed price. This highly desirable practice proved so popular that it was soon adopted by other grocers and tea-traders, many of whose names are still known today.

A contributory factor to the growing popularity of tea was the supremacy of the British at sea during the nineteenth century, when ships belonging to the East India Company transported tea from China to Britain for the tea auctions. This company, which had become very powerful, grew out of the original ships licensed by Queen Elizabeth I in 1602 to trade with the East Indies. It was often referred to as The John Company and, more bitterly, as 'the world's greatest tea monopoly', since it controlled the supply of tea as well as the market price. In 1832, however, pressure from merchants forced the government to rescind the charter. This meant that other ships could now transport tea, and in 1834 tea began to arrive from India. By 1905 India had become the biggest tea supplier in the world.

Tea also came to Britain from Ceylon (now Sri Lanka) from 1879 onwards. Originally coffee growing had been introduced into that country by the British but coffee rust destroyed the crops and tea took its place.

The Pleasure Gardens

As early as 1661 gardens were created at Vauxhall, on the south bank of the River Thames in London. In 1732 the gardens were developed further and they became extremely popular with all sections of the public and the Prince Regent, who later became George IV, was a frequent visitor with his friends. A decade later other gardens were opened in major towns throughout the country and at Ranelagh and Marylebone in London. The attractions included dancing and firework displays in the evenings together with the opportunity for apprentices, milliners and tradesmen to mingle with the elaborately dressed members of fashionable society. As tea had become the popular drink in the middle of the eighteenth century, it was served during these evening festivities.

The gardens were later opened on Saturdays and Sundays to give whole families a chance to enjoy them; on these days tea was served during the afternoon. There is no doubt that many people experienced their first taste of tea in these pleasure gardens, which over the years were frequently referred to as 'Tea Gardens'. The popularity of the gardens waned towards the middle of the nineteenth century and they were closed.

Serving Tea

The ever-growing popularity of tea meant that people needed teacups, or a complete tea service, in which to serve tea in an elegant style in their own homes. The early importers of tea brought the first teacups and teapots into Britain from China. The cups followed the Chinese design and were small handleless bowls made of stoneware or porcelain, for the Chinese had discovered the secret of making delicate porcelain. In 1702 a German firm in Meissen discovered how to make porcelain and very soon they were exporting porcelain handleless cups and complete tea sets into Britain for the wealthy. Most people, however, had to be content with glazed stoneware. In 1745 the Chelsea factory became the first British firm to produce porcelain, followed by the Worcester factory and, in subsequent years, by the leading manufacturers of porcelain and china (also developed in the early nineteenth century), such as Minton, Royal Doulton, Spode and Wedgwood.

Cups became slightly larger during the nineteenth century as tea became less expensive and they were also made with handles.

Tea caddies were of great importance. The word caddy is believed to have originated from the Malayan word 'catty'. These containers were originally made in porcelain and resembled traditional ginger jars but later were produced in silver, tortoiseshell and fine wood. Some of the caddies would contain inner bowls for the tea, and as commercial tea-blending was unknown during the eighteenth century, some of the finest tea caddies had three containers – one for black tea, one for green tea and the third to enable the hostess to blend her own tea from these two varieties. The third bowl may also have been used for sugar (an expensive commodity at that time). Due to the high price of tea many of the caddies had locks.

The Boston Tea Party

Many of the British and Dutch who crossed the Atlantic to make their homes in America took their love of tea with them and by the middle of the eighteenth century tea drinking was even more popular in that country than in Britain. By the second half of the eighteenth century relations between the American colonies and England were becoming increasingly strained, for, although religious freedom had been established, the Stamp Act of 1765, which demanded that tax stamps should be affixed to invoices and other written translations, caused so much bitter resentment and strenuous opposition among the colonists that it had to be repealed. It was, however, speedily followed by the Declaration Act which allowed the British Parliament to tax the colonists on various commodities, including tea. The Americans refused in principle to pay this tax and promptly boycotted tea from Britain and opened up a brisk trade in smuggled tea from Holland.

This meant that the East India Company, who supplied tea to America through their importers, were faced with surplus stocks. They therefore persuaded the British Government to pass the Tea Act of 1773, securing them the right to export tea directly to America without either British or American importers being involved. This ill-judged step angered both the importers, who were losing business, and the people of America, who felt their rights were being eroded.

The East India Company went ahead with their plans and transported shiploads of tea to the port of Boston. The enraged inhabitants joined with American tea importers and, disguised as native Indians, they tipped the entire cargo of tea into the sea. This event has been known ever since as the Boston Tea Party. Colonists and importers at five other ports copied their example and when ships arrived carrying tea, the cargoes were either destroyed or refused a landing.

The British Parliament retaliated with harsh measures and war resulted. It could therefore be said that tea played a vital part in the bitter War of Independence that followed. It also meant a certain decline of tea drinking in America.

Tea Clippers

The ships originally used by the East India Company to transport tea to Britain and America from China were stately and slow; a voyage could take five or six months. After the War of Independence the Americans began to build fast sailing ships to transport tea and other commodities from various countries. These ships were based on the privateers that had eluded the British navy during the war. They were given the name clippers – possibly because they 'clipped time from previous records' or 'were going at a good clip (speed)'.

The British realized they also needed faster ships and during the period 1850-1870 built a number of these three-masted, fully rigged sailing vessels. The captains and crews were chosen from mariners who enjoyed the thrill of speed and who would be capable of driving a vessel to the limit of its capacity.

Every year there was a clipper race to bring tea from China to England and the excitement was intense. Seven or eight clippers would leave Foochow on the same tide, and begin their long journey from China across the Indian and Atlantic oceans, past the Azores and into the English Channel to the port of London where tugs would bring them into harbour. A generous cash reward was bestowed on the captain and crew of the winning vessel and the tea from their ship had an enhanced value at the subsequent tea auction.

Among the famous names of the clippers were Taeping, Ariel and Cutty Sark, and the record holder Nightingale, which travelled from China to London in 91 days. The last race was in 1866.

The opening of the Suez Canal in 1869 and the advent of steam engines reduced the length of the voyages even further.

Tea Dances

The habit of enjoying tea in tea shops and cafés that began at the end of the nineteenth century encouraged ladies to entertain their friends outside their own homes. The large department stores opened restaurants at which music was provided to while away the time as the ladies sat over their afternoon tea. The fashions were formal and no lady would go out to tea without being well dressed, complete with gloves and a hat.

At the very beginning of the twentieth century afternoon tea dances became the vogue. This meant that teatime was an even longer and more leisurely affair and ladies and their male partners would dance and enjoy tea for several hours. The dresses worn for these tea dances were beautifully elegant and comfortable but without the formality of evening wear. At the beginning of the century they would have been full length but later on they became somewhat shorter. Tea gowns were made of soft fabrics like silk, chiffon or georgette and trimmed with beautiful lace or embroidery. They floated gracefully as the dancers moved. Younger ladies could feel correctly dressed without wearing a hat.

The Second World War ended this popular custom but happily tea dances are now being revived.

The Twentieth Century

The two world wars of the twentieth century confirmed the fondness of the British for their cups of tea. The rationing of many foods, including tea, made people appreciate just how essential this was for them. Every spoonful of tea was used carefully; left-over brewed tea would be strained into a clean container to be heated later or poured into a warmed vacuum flask just in case there was an air raid and one could not brew a pot of tea. How welcome tea was when the 'all clear' sounded! There was a great demand for cake recipes that did not use eggs, for these were scarce. Some of the recipes developed during this period used tea as the liquid ingredient, since it added flavour as well as an attractive colour. A typical recipe is on page 76.

Teabags grew in popularity after the Second World War and gradually one could choose from a wide variety of different blends.

The most famous tea parties in the world take place each year in London and in Scotland. Her Majesty the Queen gives three garden parties at Buckingham Palace and one at Holyrood House in Edinburgh. Thousands of distinguished people, or those who have served the country well, enjoy a delicious afternoon tea. The first recorded garden party was held at Buckingham Palace in 1868. Elizabeth II reintroduced these in 1958, when the practice of presenting débutantes at court ended.

Styles and Customs Today

Taking tea is an international custom and it is fascinating to study how tea is served in different countries and how it assumes a particular role in the life of each region.

Britain and English-speaking Countries

In these countries tea is served throughout the day. It starts with the early morning cup of tea and continues until teatime and beyond. Many people like to end the day with a cup of tea. Some people serve tea after luncheon or dinner.

While many families still pour their tea from a teapot there has been a real change towards using teabags placed straight into the cup.

Traditional British breakfast cups are large, holding approximately 1/2 pint/300 ml or the equivalent of 1 1/4 American cups. Teatime cups are smaller than breakfast cups and they generally hold just over 1/4 pint/150 ml (or two-thirds of an American cup).

Most families cherish their special-occasion porcelain or delicate china tea sets, which enhance the appearance of the tea table. The great names of English ceramics still produce wonderful tea services, which are appreciated at home and exported around the world.

Most people in Britain prefer tea with milk, rather than by itself or with lemon. The first mention of adding milk to tea appears in a travel book written in 1655 by Jean Nieuhoff (a Dutch author). He mentions that this was the practice in Canton, China.

Some years ago there was a somewhat lengthy but light-hearted enquiry as to whether it was correct (or 'U', as it was termed at the time) to pour milk into the cups before adding the tea or to pour the tea into the cups and hand the milk around, to be added as desired. Even tea experts were divided in their views. No conclusion was reached by the public, who wisely decided to do what pleased them most. In fact either method gives a good cup of tea – if the tea itself is well made.

Iced tea is a favourite in America, Australia and South Africa, where the weather can be very hot. The ideal way to prepare this is to three-quarters fill tall glasses with ice, make tea as described on page 23, allow it to brew (stand) as recommended, then strain it over the ice. This gives the flavour of freshly brewed tea and it is made icy cold in minutes.

In the farming communities of Australia and New Zealand people need to carry tea, or arrange the facilities to make tea, when they are travelling in the bush or working on their huge farms. In the *Early Settlers' Household Lore* by N. Pescott, 1977, there is an ode in praise of the billy (the container in which the water is boiled), and instructions for making 'Billy Tea':

Boil billy over the camp fire, putting a twig across the open mouth to prevent smoking. When boiling, throw in several generous spoonfuls of tea, then take the billy handle and quickly describe circles several times, so the leaves are sent to the bottom of the billy.

Wherever you are tea is wonderfully refreshing for a picnic; it is better to take the hot strained tea in one warmed vacuum flask and the cold milk in a second, chilled, vacuum flask.

China

Tea was grown in China long before it was known in any other country. It is still produced there today, both for home consumption and for export and China offers more varieties of tea than any other country. Tea is still the most popular beverage in China, for it blends so well with the food of the country. The age-old custom of serving tea to a guest on arrival has endured. Tea is drunk throughout the day and at the end of a meal. At elaborate dinners it is served throughout the meal, for tea is thought to refresh the palate and make the diners more appreciative of each course.

Perfectly made Chinese tea is crystal clear with a fine bouquet. It is taken without milk, lemon or sugar, although a little sugar may be offered, or added, if the beverage is served with sweet foods. Fresh flower or fruit blossoms are often added when brewing the tea, or in the manufacture of tea. That is why you will find tea with such exotic names as 'rose petal', jasmine', 'chrysanthemum', 'lychee' and 'plum'. Semi-fermented (oolong), green and black teas are used (although black tea is often called 'red' in China, for the tea made from this is reddish in colour).

The water for making the tea is boiled in a brass kettle, while in most homes the teapot will be of fine porcelain rather than silver for it is felt that metal imparts a 'foreign' taste to tea. The teapots are frequently encased in their own baskets, so the tea keeps hot for a considerable time.

Authentic Chinese cups have three parts: the handleless cup, a saucer and a concave lid, which serves a double purpose of keeping the tea hot and also acts as a strainer if the tea is made directly into the cup. This courteous arrangement allows everyone to enjoy their own freshly brewed tea. Teabags, now popular in China as elsewhere, simplify the process of tea making in a cup.

India

India is not only the largest producer of tea, but her inhabitants consume more tea than those of any other country. In most homes tea drinking begins first thing in the morning. In the villages and country districts a fire is lit and the water heated in a samovar, very like that used in Russia. In many parts of India the tea will be of the green type, similar to that used in Tibet and some of the tea used in China. This is sprinkled into the samovar, a little sugar added if required and the mixture heated. As the samovar is kept hot over the fire the tea can be enjoyed throughout the day. Sometimes crushed cardamom and crushed almonds are added to the tea for extra flavour. In more sophisticated houses in towns and cities, where modern appliances are available, the water will be heated in a kettle or a saucepan on the cooker.

Spiced tea (*masala chai*) is very popular. Heat the water in a saucepan with a few cloves, a small piece of cinnamon stick and 3 or 4 cardamom pods or a good pinch of ground cardamom. Bring the liquid to the boil and cover the pan. Simmer gently for about 8 minutes then add the required quantity of tea – black tea is generally used. Stir well and cover the pan. After a few minutes add milk and sugar to taste.

In some cases the milk and sugar are simmered in the spiced water before adding the tea. Strain the hot tea into cups and serve.

Sri Lanka

Tea in the beautiful island of Sri Lanka is served in a similar way to the tea in India, although in both countries the British influence means you will also be offered traditional British-style tea as well as the other varieties. The tea grown in Sri Lanka is still referred to as 'Ceylon tea'.

Japan

The Japanese tea ceremony is known as *Cha-no-yu* (tea hot-water). It is conducted with enormous precision and is based upon Sado, 'the way of tea'. *Cha-no-yu* was first practised in the eighth century and during that period was closely connected with the worship of Buddha. For the next seven centuries the elaborate ceremonies continued with the use of gold and silver utensils.

The modern *Cha-no-yu* is based upon a ritual established by tea-master Sen-no-Rikyu in the sixteenth century. His descendants opened tea ceremony schools which exist today. Young women wishing to learn the art of the tea ceremony before marriage make up the bulk of the students.

The tea room, in which the ceremony is conducted, is small, with mats on the floor. The guests gather in the outer and inner gardens outside the tea house (*sukiya*). They wash their hands and mouths in water from a stone basin in the garden before entering. The tea-master and guests use different doors; frequently the doorway for the guests will be so low that they have to crawl or bend very low to go through this. This attitude is believed to encourage humility towards the ceremony. The emotions behind the ritual are the 'Four Principles' of harmony, reverence, purity and tranquillity.

A scroll hangs in the tea house and the guests are expected to pay their respects to this before they sit along the east side of the room to wait for the tea-master, who is their tea-host. Before the tea ritual begins a light meal of soup, pickles and other delicacies is served. The guests are then invited to retire to the inner garden until summoned back by the striking of a gong. After purifying their hands and mouths again, they return to the tea room to find the scroll replaced by a vase of flowers, and the tea utensils, which have been laid out by the tea-host. There is the beautiful tea container, kept in a silk bag, and the scoop for spooning the tea into the bowl. Nowadays this is generally made of bamboo, while earlier ones were of ivory. There is a white cloth for wiping the bowl, the exquisite bowl itself and a very fine bamboo whisk. There will also be a pitcher of water and a ladle for the water.

Japanese green tea (*matcha*) that has been steamed, dried and ground to a powder, is used for the ceremony. The kettle of water may be heated on a hearth sunk in the floor or on a ceramic stand over a brazier. The powdered tea is placed in the bowl, the water from the kettle added and the tea whisked until foamy. It is passed to the first guest with the part of the bowl with the most beautiful design on it towards him or her. Tradition decrees that the guest takes the bowl in the right hand, rotates it with the left hand clockwise, drinks a little tea, wipes the bowl, rotates it clockwise once more and passes it to the next guest. After the end of the first ceremony the guests may handle the utensils themselves.

A second tea ceremony begins, using a thinner tea (*usucha*). The complete *Cha-no-yu* can last for between three and four hours.

Arab Countries

Mint tea is an important beverage in the Arab countries of Africa, Egypt, Libya, Morocco, the Maghreb and Sudan. Although available in all Arab countries, it is less popular in those east of Suez. In some countries it is served both before and after a meal, while in others it is customary to finish a meal, rinse mouths and hands and then relax over the mint tea.

In affluent homes the teapot is made of silver plate, while poorer people would use pottery or china. Green tea is generally used (see page 8) and great attention is paid to the quality of the mint, dark green mint or spearmint being the favourites. In summer orange blossom may be added to the mint and in winter, if mint is not available, sage, sweet marjoram or sweet basil will be substituted.

To make mint tea, boil the water, rinse out the teapot and throw this away. Put in the required amount of tea, a handful of mint leaves (or the alternative) plus about 1 oz/25 g (2 tablespoons) cane sugar; the tea is always very sweet. Pour on boiling water and let it brew (stand) for at least 3 minutes. Stir just once or twice, then pour into glasses. Add more sugar if required.

When shopping in Arab countries you may well be invited to partake of mint tea as you bargain with the retailer, for this is an accepted part of the purchasing process, which can take a considerable time.

USSR

Tea is one of the national beverages in Russia and few homes are without a samovar – the traditional, and well-loved, receptacle for boiling water in for making the tea. When the tea is brewed the pot is placed on top of the samovar to keep the tea hot. In the past the samovar was heated by charcoal but nowadays electric models are available.

In Russia many people drink tea with, or after, a meal. The usual way of drinking tea is to pour a little from the teapot into a glass or cup then fill this with boiling water from the samovar. Tea is generally served with slices of lemon and it is quite commonplace to have a spoonful of blackcurrant or other jam to sweeten the tea instead of sugar.

In the vast expanse of the USSR you will find various regional customs associated with tea drinking. The Buryats, from eastern Siberia, serve green tea at the start of a meal with bread or biscuits and butter. Only after this is the meat dish brought in. The name of the Buryat green tea is *nogoon sai*. It is boiled in water before cream or milk is added, and the liquid is then allowed to simmer for a short time. It is then salted.

In the region which was originally Astrakhan, the Kalmyks follow the same method of making tea as the Buryats but they also add pepper and a little clarified butter.

By the camp fire in Siberia, no conversation takes place without tea. In the north the distance covered in a day is measured in terms of the number of tea breaks needed.

Tibet

In the book *Tibet is My Country* written by Heinrich Harrer, the elder brother of the Dalai Lama describes the tea he enjoyed at home when he was a young child before he went into the monastery to begin the training for his future life:

> Our first tea of the day was drunk at breakfast. It was always mildly exciting to watch the water beginning to boil in the copper kettle, and then see mother break a piece off from the tea brick, rub it between her palms and then throw the curling leaves into the bubbling water. After that she would add a little salt and then let the tea boil for a moment or two.
> In our province the Amdo people used dried tea leaves pressed into bricks which were imported from China throughout the province of Kham. It was a rather coarse kind of tea, and these bricks often contained whole leaves, and sometimes even stalks.

He recalls that later in the day the children could sometimes wheedle their mother into allowing them to add a little butter to their tea. This is a custom still followed in Tibet.

Choosing and Using Tea

There are so many teas on sale today that the choice is almost limitless. Most people find the particular make of tea they prefer and buy this regularly – for they know that the care taken by the tea-tasters and blenders will ensure its consistent quality. Even if you have a favourite tea it is worthwhile experimenting from time to time by buying some of the speciality teas; these all have their own individual flavour. Some of the most readily available are given below and on page 22.

Blended teas account for practically 90% of all tea sold in Britain. Blending tea has been described by a tea expert as a 'work of art' for, in order to achieve the desired flavour, the most careful selection of a great variety of different teas has to be made. After this the blender must choose the right proportion of each tea to achieve the desired result.

The serving suggestions given with the following teas are a guide only; there are no hard and fast rules for when to serve each type of tea, and as all tea lovers know, anytime is teatime.

Indian teas

Darjeeling is grown in the foothills of the Himalayas and is often known as the Champagne of Teas, with its muscatel flavour. It is a good breakfast tea.

Assam is a full-bodied tea with a rich malty flavour. It makes a refreshing drink on a hot day, and is often favoured at breakfast or mid-morning.

Nilgiri produces a light mild-flavoured tea that is perfect for serving after a delicate meal.

Ceylon (Sri Lankan) teas

Dimbula has a fine flavour and a golden colour, and makes a refreshing mid-morning drink.

Nuwara Eliya is a light tea with a delicate taste that is excellent served with lemon or iced.

Kandy is a tea of full-bodied flavour that is ideal as a breakfast, mid-morning or iced drink.

Uva has a pungent flavour and rosy-coloured liquor. It is used extensively for blending.

China teas

Jasmine tea contains real jasmine flowers. It is light and refreshing and makes a soothing late-night drink. It is traditionally served with the meal in Chinese restaurants.

Keemun is a black tea which the Chinese say 'has the fragrance of an orchid'. Serve with Chinese food or after a meal of white meat or fish.

Lapsang Souchong has a distinctive tarry aroma and smoky taste and should not be taken with milk. Serve after a strong-flavoured meal.

Formosa oolong is the most expensive of all teas. It is semi-fermented, and has a very delicate flavour of peach blossom. Rose-flavoured oolongs are also available. Serve oolongs after a white meat or fish meal, or as a late-night drink.

Kenyan teas

Tea from Kenya is not only an important ingredient in blended teas but is also sold as a speciality tea. These produce a full-bodied, coppery-coloured beverage that is ideal for the first drink of the day.

Special blends

Earl Grey is one of the best-known speciality teas. It is named after the second Earl Grey who so delighted a Chinese Mandarin with his praise of tea that the blend was created in his honour. It is traditionally a combination of black China and Indian Darjeeling teas, flavoured with oil of bergamot (a small tree of the citrus family). Hot or iced, it is a favourite afternoon tea and is ideal for entertaining or special occasions.

English Breakfast tea can vary from blend to blend, but it is usually Indian and Ceylon teas blended to produce a full-flavoured brew.

Herb teas

For centuries herbs have been used to make various flavoured teas; although in the past the beverage was often referred to as a tisane or a potion. There are two ways in which herbs can be used to make a refreshing and unusual flavoured drink. The first method is to add a small quantity of the selected herb (fresh or dried) to the tea leaves when brewing the tea, in the same way as when making mint tea (see page 19); the second method is to follow the directions for making tea as on page 23, substituting herbs for tea leaves. You can also buy packets of herb-flavoured teas. Many herb teas are improved by the addition of a little lemon juice, and honey makes a good sweetener.

If you find the flavour of the herb teas bitter it may be that you have let the beverage brew for too long; most herbs need a maximum of 5 minutes' standing time. Herb teas can be served iced or hot.

Some of the most suitable and readily available herbs to use for tea are:

balm (often called lemon balm); basil*; bay**; borage; caraway (use the seeds); chamomile (use the flower heads); elder (use the young flower heads); fenugreek* (use the seeds and only the young leaves); feverfew**; hyssop; lemon verbena; lovage; juniper (use the berries); mint (particularly apple mint, peppermint and spearmint); rosemary; sage; tansy; tarragon; thyme (particularly lemon thyme).

*the leaves are strongly flavoured so should be used sparingly.

**the leaves are very strongly flavoured so use very sparingly until you are sure you like the taste.

In addition to the plants known as herbs you can use cultivated plants too – rose or marigold petals make an excellent flavouring for tea, as do the leaves of rose geraniums.

A Perfect Cup of Tea

Buy the best-quality tea you can afford. Try different varieties of tea to make a change; some of the most interesting types are on pages 21-22.

Tea loses flavour when exposed to the air, so when you open a packet transfer the tea to an airtight container. Teabags should be treated in the same way.

Always take fresh water from the cold tap; this makes a surprising difference to the taste of the tea.

Just before the water comes to the boil, pour some into the teapot to warm it. Pour out all the water when the teapot is thoroughly heated.

Add the amount of tea required – the old saying 'one teaspoon per person and one for the pot' is generally right, although some tea experts recommend one teaspoon per cup.

Pour the water over the tea as soon as it comes to the boil. Cover and wait for 3 minutes or a little longer if using tea with a fairly large leaf.

The tea is now ready to pour. You can strain it into the cups or pour straight from the teapot.

Serve with milk or lemon, and sugar, or try the tea just by itself.

Tea Served
Hot, Cold and Frozen

———————

'Some sipping punch, some sipping tea'

William Wordsworth (1770-1850)

As well as being the beverage enjoyed throughout the world,
tea is an essential ingredient in some hot and cold punches, wine and fruit cups.
Tea adds special interest to unusual iced desserts (see pages 42 to 45).
It is an excellent partner to alcohol, making the brew less potent,
which is an important consideration for drivers.
Tea enlivens non-alcoholic drinks, bringing out the various flavours.
Sometimes the choice and strength of tea is given in recipes but this is really a
matter of personal taste and you can of course use your favourite blended tea.
The presentation of punches and fruit and wine cups
is important, they should be a focal point on the table. Punch bowls are not
unduly expensive, but a strong cut-glass bowl could be used instead.
A long-handled silver ladle is ideal for serving the punch.
Warm or chill the bowl, whichever is appropriate,
before adding the hot mixture or the ice. Be equally careful when filling glasses,
punch cups or beakers, and insert a spoon in the container
before adding very hot liquids. Mixtures should not be boiled once the wine or
spirits have been added; you will destroy the alcohol.
Never heat a drink containing alcohol in the microwave
as it could ignite and cause a fire.
Wash citrus fruits before using the peel and discard any white pith.

To crush ice, put ice cubes in a clean cloth, crush with an ice hammer,
an ordinary hammer, a weight or a heavy rolling pin.

To frost glasses, dip the rims of the glasses in cold water or lemon juice then in
caster sugar or sifted icing sugar; leave to chill well.

Mulled Wine

This is one of the traditional Christmas drinks, dispensed to carol-singers as they
wound their way from house to house.
In the old days a red-hot poker would be plunged into the bowl
of spiced wine to make it hot.
Choose a robust and hearty wine – your wine merchant will advise you.

To heat the punch bowl, fill it with hot, not boiling, water and leave to stand. Slice the lemons very thinly and remove the pips. Put all the ingredients into a pan set over a moderate heat and heat almost to boiling point. Meanwhile, pour the hot water out of the punch bowl and dry it well. Transfer the mulled wine to the bowl. Leave to stand briefly to let the sediment settle. Add the pieces of apple and serve.

Makes 8-10 glasses

2 lemons

$3/4$ pint/450 ml (2 cups) moderately strong tea, such as Darjeeling or Kenyan, well strained

$1/2$ teaspoon ground cloves or ground nutmeg

1 or 2 cinnamon sticks about 2 inches/5 cm in length

4 oz/100 g ($1/2$ cup) caster (granulated) or light brown sugar

2 pints/1.2 litres (5 cups) red wine

To decorate

2 dessert apples, neatly diced

Apple Tea Toddy

A toddy is a comforting remedy if you have a cold. The apple purée can be made from cooked fruit or liquidized fresh fruit.
Serve in a thick beaker so you can warm your hands while sipping the drink.

Makes 1 beaker

2 tablespoons (2 1/2 tbsp) apple purée

1/4 pint/150 ml (2/3 cup) moderately strong tea, such as Assam, well strained

a good measure of whisky

sugar or honey to taste

Place the apple purée in a jug, add the tea and leave to stand for 5 minutes. Strain the apple-flavoured tea into a small saucepan and heat to boiling point. Add a good measure of whisky. Heat the liquid through, but do not let it boil. Stir in a little sugar or honey and serve.

Brandy Lemon Punch

This is a simple but luxurious hot punch.

Makes 8-10 glasses

1 pint/600 ml (2 1/2 cups) moderately strong tea, such as Kandy, well strained

4 tablespoons (5 tbsp) lemon juice

3 oz/75 g (3/8 cup) caster (granulated) sugar

1/2 pint/300 ml (1 1/4 cups) brandy

To decorate

lemon slices

Pour the hot tea into a saucepan and add the lemon juice and sugar. Heat together, stirring occasionally, until the sugar has completely dissolved. Add the brandy and heat the liquid through, but do not let it boil. To serve, transfer the punch to a preheated bowl and top with lemon slices.

Oxford Punch

Port wine, together with orange and tea, makes a wonderfully
rich-flavoured hot drink.
It is important to use a really dark bitter marmalade.

Press 3 cloves into each orange; if the pieces of peel in the marmalade are rather large chop them finely. Put the oranges, marmalade and tea into a saucepan and heat to boiling point. Add the port wine and heat the liquid through, without letting it boil. To serve, transfer to a preheated bowl and top with grated nutmeg, if liked.

Makes 12-14 glasses

6 cloves

2 oranges

8 oz/225 g (scant 3/4 cup) bitter marmalade

1 pint/600 ml (2 1/2 cups) moderately strong tea, such as Assam or Dimbula, well strained

2 bottles port wine

a little grated or ground nutmeg, optional

If you are cold tea will warm you. If you are heated it will cool you.
If you are depressed it will cheer you. If you are excited it will calm you.

William Ewart Gladstone (1809-1898) four times Prime Minister of Britain

Sherry Posset

Ground almonds are an interesting and very long-established way of adding
a little thickening to liquids.
Take great care the mixture does not boil; it will curdle and affect
the texture of the ground almonds.

Makes 8-10 glasses

1 pint/600 ml (2 1/2 cups) weak
tea, such as Nuwara Eliya,
well strained

2 oz/50 g (1/2 cup) ground
almonds

1 1/2 pints/900 ml (3 3/4 cups)
milk

1/2 pint/300 ml (1 1/4 cups)
sweet sherry sugar to taste

Pour the tea into a saucepan, add the ground almonds and milk and
bring almost to boiling point. Stir in the sherry and heat gently. Add
sugar to taste. Serve in warmed glasses.

Winter Cordial

A cordial is by definition a sweetened drink.
This one is a warming thick drink that is ideal for frosty nights.

Makes 6-8 glasses

1 large lemon

2 tablespoons (2 1/2 tbsp) rolled
oats

2 tablespoons (2 1/2 tbsp)
demerara (light brown) sugar

1 1/2 pints/900 ml (3 3/4 cups)
strong tea, such as Darjeeling
or Kenyan, well strained

1/4 pint/150 ml (2/3 cup)
whisky or dark rum

Finely grate the lemon rind and squeeze out the juice. Put the lemon
rind, rolled oats, sugar and hot tea into a saucepan. Bring the mixture
to the boil. Add the lemon juice and simmer for 5 minutes, stirring all
the time. Strain the liquid and return it to the saucepan. Add the
whisky or rum and heat the liquid through, but do not let it boil. Serve
in warmed glasses.

Melon Wine Cup

The good flavour of this drink is achieved by leaving
the melon, wine and tea to stand for some hours in the refrigerator
so that the flavours will blend and intensify.

Halve the melon. Scoop out the seeds and any pulp adhering to them and place in a bowl with the lemon juice, hot tea and sugar. Leave until absolutely cold. Strain the tea, which will have absorbed the flavour from the melon seeds, into the punch bowl. Discard the seeds. Cut the melon flesh into tiny balls with a potato scoop or dice very neatly. Put the melon balls or cubes into the punch bowl with the cold tea. Add the wine and mint sprigs. Cover and chill for several hours. Ice is not necessary in this drink.

To Make a Change
Melon Orange Wine Cup. Omit the lemon juice. Use only 1 bottle of white wine plus 3/4 pint/450 ml (2 cups) of orange juice. You may not require any sugar in this recipe.

Makes 12 glasses

1 ripe honeydew melon

2 tablespoons (2 1/2 tbsp) lemon juice

1 pint/600 ml (2 1/2 cups) China tea, such as Lapsang Souchong or rose-flavoured tea, well strained

2 tablespoons (2 1/2 tbsp) caster (granulated) sugar

1 1/2 bottles moderately dry white wine, well chilled

a few mint sprigs

Strawberry Cup

The true flavour of strawberries makes this lightly fizzy drink ideal for a summer party.

Makes 12 glasses

1 lb/450 g (1 lb) small ripe strawberries

1 pint/600 ml (2 1/2 cups) China tea, such as Formosa Oolong or Lapsong Souchong, well strained

2 tablespoons (2 1/2 tbsp) lemon juice

2 tablespoons (2 1/2 tbsp) caster (granulated) sugar

a little crushed ice

1 bottle rosé wine, well chilled

1/2 pint/300 ml (1 1/4 cups) soda water

To decorate

mint sprigs

Press just over half the strawberries through a sieve into a bowl. Add the hot tea, lemon juice and sugar and leave to cool.

Put the ice into a punch bowl, a cut glass bowl or a jug. Add the strawberry tea mixture, then the wine. Top with the whole strawberries and mint sprigs. Pour in the soda water just before serving.

To Make a Change

Use raspberries or loganberries instead of strawberries. Loganberries could be simmered for a few minutes in the tea and lemon juice to make them a little more tender. As this fruit is more acid increase the amount of sugar to 4 oz/100 g (1/2 cup).

Summer Peach Punch

This summer drink looks beautifully cool and refreshing.
Add the lemon juice and tea immediately after slicing the peaches so the fruit
does not discolour.

Immerse the peaches in boiling water for a few seconds, remove and peel away the skins. Halve the fruit, remove the stones and cut the flesh into thin slices. Place the peach slices in a bowl. Add the lemon juice, hot tea and sugar and leave to cool.

Place the ice in a punch bowl. Add the peach slices in their liquid and then the wine. Top with the borage flowers and cherries.

Makes 12 glasses

3 large ripe peaches

2 tablespoons (2 1/2 tbsp) lemon juice

3/4 pint/450 ml (2 cups) weak tea, such as Dimbula, well strained

2 tablespoons (2 1/2 tbsp) caster (granulated) sugar

a little crushed ice

1 bottle white wine, well chilled

To decorate

borage flowers

a few black cherries, stoned

Rum and Lemon Cup

The refreshing flavours combined in this delicious drink make it
an ideal choice for a hot day.

Makes 10-12 glasses

1 pint/600 ml (2 1/2 cups) weak
China tea, such as Lapsong
Souchong, well strained

4 medium lemons

1/2 pint/300 ml (1 1/4 cups)
water

4 oz/100 g (1/2 cup) caster
(granulated) or light brown
sugar

1/2 pint/300 ml (1 1/4 cups) rum

a little crushed ice

1/2 pint/300 ml (1 1/4 cups)
soda or tonic water

To decorate

1 or 2 lemons, thinly sliced

thin slices of cucumber

borage sprigs

Leave the tea to become quite cold. Pare the top zest from the lemons and place it in a saucepan with the water. Simmer for 8 minutes. Add the sugar and stir until dissolved. Strain the liquid into a bowl and leave to cool.

Squeeze the juice from the lemons and add it to the cold lemon-flavoured water with the cold tea and the rum. Chill in the refrigerator.

To serve, put a little crushed ice into the chilled serving bowl. Blend the soda or tonic water with the rum mixture and pour over the ice. Top with the lemon and cucumber slices and borage.

Christmas Champagne Cup

This is a splendid cold drink for a Christmas party.
Imitate the bright colours of seasonal decorations with the cherries and other fruits.

Peel the zest from the lemon and 2 of the oranges and place in a saucepan with the tea and sugar. Bring to the boil, stirring to dissolve the sugar. Remove the pan from the heat and leave to cool. Strain the tea and pour it into ice-making trays. Put a whole or halved cherry into each of the sections so they will be in the centre of each cube.

Squeeze the juice from the lemon and oranges. Put the tea-flavoured ice cubes in the bowl. Blend the fruit juices with the Curaçao or brandy and pour over the ice cubes. Add the champagne and scatter tangerine segments and grapes on top.

Makes 12 glasses

1 lemon

3 oranges

1 pint/600 ml (2 1/2 cups) weak tea, such as Dimbula or Nilgiri, well strained

2 oz/50 g (4 tbsp) caster (granulated) sugar

maraschino or glacé (candied) cherries

1/4 pint/150 ml (2/3 cup) Curaçao or brandy

2 bottles champagne

To decorate

tangerine segments

a few black and white grapes

Spiced Tea

The cinnamon, cloves and orange give this drink a haunting aroma.

Makes 8 glasses

3/4 pint/450 ml (2 cups) water

2 inches/5 cm cinnamon stick

3 cloves

3 oz/75 g (3/8 cup) caster (granulated) sugar

1 1/2 pints/900 ml (3 3/4 cups) moderately strong tea, such as Assam or Earl Grey, well strained

1/4 pint/150 ml (2/3 cup) orange juice

Put the water into a saucepan with the cinnamon, cloves and sugar. Heat to boiling point. Add the hot tea and orange juice. Bring just to boiling point again. Remove the cinnamon stick and cloves and serve in warmed glasses.

Ginger Punch

This is an ideal hot drink for teenagers – it has plenty of flavour but no alcohol, and looks attractive with the lemon slices and diced ginger on top.

Makes 8-10 glasses

1/2 pint/300 ml (1 1/4 cups) weak tea, such as Kandy, well strained

1 lemon, sliced and pips removed

2 oz/50 g (1/3 cup) preserved ginger, diced finely

2 oz/50 g (4 tbsp) brown sugar

2 pints/1.2 litres (5 cups) ginger ale or ginger beer

Pour the hot tea into a saucepan. Add the lemon slices, diced ginger, sugar and ginger ale or beer. Heat, but do not boil. Serve in warmed glasses.

Honey Apple Punch

This is an excellent drink for cold weather.
As most apple juice is rather sweet the quantity of honey in the recipe is fairly low.
The choice of apples affects the flavour:
cooking (baking) apples make it sharper, dessert apples add sweetness.
A little lemon juice adds extra tang if you like it.

Core, but do not peel the apples and cut them into neat slices. Place in a saucepan with the apple juice, honey, tea and lemon juice, if used, and heat to boiling point. Do not continue cooking or the fruit will soften and make the drink cloudy. Serve in warmed glasses with the slices of apple on top, and a sprinkling of ground cinnamon, if liked.

To Make a Change
Ginger Apple Punch. Use 1 pint/600 ml (2½ cups) ginger ale with 1 pint/600 ml (2½ cups) apple juice, 1 pint/600 ml (2½/2 cups) China tea (as above) and the same quantity of honey and sliced apples.

Makes 10 glasses

2 small apples (see method for preparation)

2 pints/1.2 litres (5 cups) apple juice

2 tablespoons (2 ½ tbsp) honey

1 pint/600 ml (2 ½ cups) China tea, such as Keemun, well strained

lemon juice, optional

a sprinkling of ground cinnamon, optional

'Look here, Steward, if this is coffee, I want tea; but if this is tea,
then I wish for coffee.'

Punch 1902

Lemon Punch

This hot punch has a really lively flavour.
The amount of sugar can be adjusted depending on whether you prefer
a sharp or sweet taste.

Makes 10 glasses

4 large or 5 small lemons

1/2 pint/300 ml (1 1/4 cups)
   water

2 inches/5 cm cinnamon stick

a pinch of ground cardamom

4 oz/100 g (1/2 cup) caster
   (granulated) sugar

2 pints/1.2 litres (5 cups) weak
   tea, such as Jasmine, well
   strained

Pare the zest from 2 lemons and cut it into matchstick strips. Place in a saucepan with the water, cinnamon stick, cardamom and sugar. Bring to the boil, remove from the heat and leave to stand for 30 minutes.

Squeeze the juice from the lemons and add it to the cinnamon-flavoured water with the tea. Heat through without boiling. To serve, remove the cinnamon stick and pour into a warmed bowl or individual glasses.

Iced Tea Punch

This pretty summer drink is perfect for a party.
Give each guest a teaspoon in order to eat the fruit.

Remove the pips from the lemon slices and place them in a bowl. Peel the pineapple and cut out the hard centre core. Place the core (which has quite a lot of flavour) into the bowl with the lemon slices. Dice the pineapple flesh neatly and set aside. Pour the very hot tea over the lemon slices and pineapple core and leave to cool completely. Strain. Blend the lemon juice, pineapple juice and strained cold tea together. Put the ice cubes into the punch bowl and pour in the tea mixture. Add the diced fresh pineapple. Add the bitter lemon or lemonade and decorate with strawberries, borage flowers and cucumber slices just before serving.

Makes 12 glasses

1 lemon, sliced

1 small pineapple

1 1/2 pints/900 ml (3 3/4 cups) moderately strong tea, such as Earl Grey or Kenyan, well strained

1/4 pint/150 ml (2/3 cup) lemon juice

1 pint/600 ml (2 1/2 cups) pineapple juice

ice cubes

1 1/2 pints/900 ml (3 3/4 cups) bitter lemon or sparkling lemonade

To decorate

a few small strawberries or raspberries

borage or elderberry flowers

wafer-thin cucumber slices

Tea, although an Oriental,
Is a gentleman at least;
Cocoa is a cad and coward
Cocoa is a vulgar beast.

The Song of Right and Wrong, G. K. Chesterton (1874-1936)

Creamy Tea Shake

In this milk shake tea provides a good contrast to the sweetness of the ice cream.
Use your favourite type of tea.

Makes 1 glass

1/2 tumbler of tea, well strained and chilled

1/4 tumbler of milk

1 scoop vanilla ice cream

Place the tea, milk and ice cream in a liquidizer or blender. Blend briefly until light and fluffy. Serve at once.

To Make a Change

Hot Cream Tea Shake. Blend together hot tea, hot milk and a generous tablespoon of single (light) cream. Top with a light dusting of brown sugar.

Frosted Citrus Tea

Serve this drink on long, hot summer days.
The lightly frozen tea and fruit mixture is very refreshing.

Makes 10-12 glasses

1 pint/600 ml (2 1/2 cups) moderately strong tea, such as Assam or Dimbula, well strained and chilled

1 pint/600 ml (2 1/2 cups) unsweetened orange juice

1 pint/600 ml (2 1/2 cups) unsweetened grapefruit juice

2 tablespoons (2 1/2 tbsp) lemon juice

a little sifted icing (confectioners') sugar

To decorate

orange slices

lemon slices

Blend the cold tea with the fruit juices. Pour into a container and place in the freezer or freezing compartment of the refrigerator. Leave until the first ice crystals form. Blend in a little icing sugar, which not only sweetens the mixture but enhances the frosted effect.

Spoon into tall glasses and top with orange and lemon slices.

Orange Fizz

This is a drink that children will enjoy,
with the chink of ice cubes and the orange slices. The addition of a small amount
of tea prevents it from being oversweet.

Combine the cold tea with the orange juice. Put the ice cubes into tall glasses and half-fill them with the orange and tea mixture. Top up with orangeade. To serve, make a slit in the orange slices and balance them on the rims of the glasses or float on top of the drink.

To Make a Change
Serve with small strawberries on top instead of orange slices.

Ice Cream and Orange Fizz. Follow the method above, but do not fill the glasses to the top with the orangeade. Top each glass with a spoonful of vanilla ice cream. Serve with a spoon as well as straws.

Makes 6-8 glasses

$1/2$ pint/300 ml (1 $1/4$ cups) weak tea, such as Keemun or Lapsong Souchong, well strained and chilled

$1/4$ pint/150 ml ($2/3$ cup) orange juice

ice cubes

$1 1/2$ pints/900 ml (3 $3/4$ cups) fizzy orangeade

To decorate

6-8 orange slices

If a stranger say unto thee
That he thirsteth
Give him a cup of tea.

Confucius (551-479 BC)

Tea Ice Cream

This ice cream is ideal for people who like a sharp-flavoured dessert.

Serves 6

3 teaspoons tea (choose a type that gives a fairly strong brew), such as Assam or Kandy

$1/2$ pint/300 ml (1 $1/4$ cups) water

2 small or 1 large lemon

3 eggs

3 oz/75 g ($3/8$ cup) caster (granulated) sugar

$1/2$ pint/300 ml (1 $1/4$ cups) double (heavy) cream

Place the tea in a clean, warmed pot or jug. Bring the water to the boil and pour it over the tea. Add the thinly pared rind from the lemon(s) (do not use any of the white pith). Stir well, and allow to stand for 5 minutes. Strain very carefully.

Separate the eggs. Beat the yolks in a heatproof bowl with half the sugar. Add the strained lemon-flavoured tea and stand the bowl over a pan of very hot, but not boiling, water. Whisk briskly until the mixture thickens. Cool slightly, and add about 1 tablespoon (1 $1/4$ tablespoons) of lemon juice. Whisk the mixture from time to time as it cools.

Whip the cream until it just holds its shape and blend with the cold tea mixture. Turn into a freezer-proof container and freeze lightly until the ice cream just holds its shape.

Whisk the egg whites until they stand in peaks. Fold in the remaining sugar, and blend with the lightly frozen ice cream. Return to the container and freeze until firm.

This ice cream is particularly good served with segments of fresh orange and sliced kiwi fruit or sliced fresh pineapple.

Maraschino Mallow

Ice cream based upon marshmallows is particularly light and easy to make.
Tea gives an unusual and subtle taste
to the mixture and prevents it being oversweet.

Allow the tea to infuse for 5 minutes, then strain thoroughly. Put the marshmallows into a basin and pour over the hot tea. Place the basin over a pan of hot water and leave until the marshmallows have just melted. (This may also be done in a microwave oven.) Chill the mixture well.

Add the cherries and maraschino syrup to the marshmallows; spoon into a container and freeze lightly. Whip the cream until it just stands in peaks but do not overwhip. Fold the cream into the lightly frozen mixture, and freeze until firm. Remove the ice cream from the freezer about 15 minutes before serving; it is nicer if it is not too firm.

This can be stored in the freezer for up to one month without losing its light texture.

Serves 4-6

1/4 pint/150 ml (2/3 cup) freshly brewed tea, such as Kandy

6 oz/75 g (1 1/2 cups) marshmallows

2 oz/50 g (1/4 cup) maraschino cherries, quartered

2 tablespoons (2 1/2 tbsp) marashino syrup

1/2 pint/300 ml (1 1/4 cups) double (heavy) cream

Rose Petal Ice Cream

This is a delicious blending of unusual flavours.

Strain the hot tea into a liquidizer. Add the sugar and rose petals. Process to make a smooth purée. Turn into a container. Chill then freeze lightly. Whip the cream until it just stands in peaks. Fold into the rose petal purée and freeze until firm.

Serves 6

1/4 pint/150 ml (2/3 cup) hot China tea, such as Keemun or rose-flavoured tea

50 g/2 oz (1/4 cup) caster (granulated) sugar

1/2 pint/300 ml (1 1/4 cups) fresh red rose petals

1/2 pint/300 ml (1 1/4 cups) double (heavy) cream

Iced Apricot Soufflé

The addition of tea to this soufflé counteracts the over-rich and insipid flavour
of many iced desserts.
The full flavour of the dried apricots is apparent, as they are softened,
but not cooked.

Serves 6-8

6 oz/175 g (1 cup) dried
apricots

3/4 pint/450 ml (2 cups) boiling
water

3 teaspoons China tea, such as
Jasmine or Lapsong
Souchong

3 oz/75 g (3/8 cup) light brown
sugar

1 tablespoon (1 1/4 tbsp) lemon
juice

3/4 pint/450 ml (2 cups) double
(heavy) cream

To decorate

2 tablespoons (2 1/2 tbsp)
pistachio nuts, skinned and
chopped

Prepare a 6 inch/15 cm soufflé dish by tying round a deep band of
lightly buttered paper so it stands about 3 inches/7.5 cm above the
top rim.

Put the apricots into a basin. Pour the boiling water over the tea and
leave to infuse for 5 minutes. Strain the hot tea over the apricots. Add
the sugar and the lemon juice. Place a small plate over the fruit so it
remains well covered with liquid; leave for 12 hours.

Liquidize the apricots and any liquid not absorbed by the fruit. Whip
the cream until it stands in peaks and put a little on one side for
decoration. Fold the remaining cream into the apricot purée.

Spoon into the soufflé dish and freeze. Remove from the freezer 15
minutes before serving. Take off the paper band. Decorate the iced
soufflé with the reserved whipped cream and pistachios.

This iced dessert can be stored in the freezer for up to two months.

To Make a Change

Iced Prune Soufflé. Substitute 6 oz/175 g (1 cup) dried prunes for the
apricots. Cook the prunes in 3/4 pint/450 ml (2 cups) of your
favourite blended tea or Earl Grey tea (see below). Substitute 2
tablespoons (2 1/2 tbsp) port wine for the lemon juice.

Individual Soufflés. Spoon the mixture into about 8 individual soufflé
dishes and freeze.

Cooking Dried Fruit

Tea imparts a delicious flavour to dried fruit, particularly prunes and
figs. Use fairly strong tea for these fruits, but choose a weak China tea
for apricots, peaches and dried apple rings. The tea should be freshly
brewed and well strained. Pour over the fruit then soak and cook in
the usual way.

Grapefruit and Mint Granita

A granita is a type of water ice that forms ice crystals
during freezing. This makes it particularly refreshing for a dessert
or an hors-d'oeuvre.

Allow the tea to infuse for 5 minutes. Strain it over the mint leaves and sugar and leave until quite cool. Strain again and blend with the grapefruit juice. Freeze lightly, then spoon into frosted glasses and top with the mint sprigs. Serve immediately.

To Make a Change

Wine and Tea Granita. Substitute 1/2 pint/300 ml (11/4 cups) rosé wine for the grape fruit juice in the recipe above. Omit the mint leaves, flavouring the hot tea with strips of lemon or orange rind. Use only the top zest and avoid any bitter white pith. Decorate with orange or lemon slices.

Tea and Yoghurt Granita. Substitute 1/2 pint/300 ml (11/4 cups) natural yoghurt for the grapefruit juice in the recipe above. Decorate the lightly frozen mixture with a mixture of fresh seasonal fruits.

Serves 4

1/2 pint/300 ml (1 1/4 cups)
   freshly brewed Ceylon tea,
   such as Nuwara Eliya

about 20 young mint leaves

3 oz/75 g (good 1/3 cup) caster
   (granulated) sugar

1/2 pint/300 ml (1 1/4 cups)
   grapefruit juice

To decorate

sprigs of mint

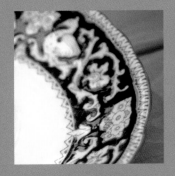  

Teatime

'Now for the tea of our host, Now for the rollicking bun,
Now for the muffin and toast, Now for the gay Sally Lunn.'

Trial by Jury

Gilbert and Sullivan

For generations teatime has been one of the most popular meals of the day,
no matter what the season.
In winter you can enjoy hot toast, toasted scones or muffins
with cakes around the fire, and when summer comes
take tea in the garden with cucumber sandwiches and cherry tarts.
Every part of Britain has its own
excellent traditional teatime recipes, ranging from interesting breads
to light cakes and pastries.

Dried fruit has long been used in British recipes, brought to the islands with
spices and silks by our merchant seamen.
Pastry has been made in Britain for hundreds of years; Chaucer mentions
it in *The Canterbury Tales*.
Cakes were originally based on a bread dough, but, as raising agents and lighter
flour became available, a wider variety of cakes was created.
This chapter traces the development of teatime as an important feature
of the day and gives a range of recipes from Britain
and other countries that share this love of a good cup of tea in the afternoon.

Hotels who had allowed their teatime menus to languish
have now discovered how much their guests enjoy a good tea, and are presenting
sumptuous spreads to tempt them.
A traditional tea is a wonderful way to entertain at home, too.
The baking and food preparations,
such as making sandwiches, can be done ahead, so you can relax
and enjoy the occasion.
Part of the pleasure of tea is its presentation: a cherished tablecloth,
pretty china cups, old-fashioned cake stands
and linen napkins will all enhance the sense of occasion.
Yet teatime is informal:
you can sit round the fireside or in the garden.

Good Baking

The secrets of success in baking the recipes in the following chapters can be summed up quite simply:

* Take the trouble to weigh or measure ingredients carefully. There must be the right balance of the flour, fat and other ingredients. Choose the type of flour, etc., that is recommended in the recipe.

* Follow the directions regarding the method of mixing the ingredients, for these are important. Words like 'folding' and 'whisking' occur in recipes. Folding is a gentle flicking and turning movement; a more vigorous action could spoil the texture of the mixture. Beating and whisking, on the other hand, are brisk energetic actions.

* Follow the baking instructions given but be aware that ovens vary slightly; so use the knowledge of your oven, acquired through experience, and adjust the temperature if necessary.

* Use the right sized tin (pan) where possible. For example, if the recipe states an 8 inch/20 cm cake tin, and you substitute a 9 inch/23 cm tin you are spreading the mixture over a wider area. As a result the cooking time will be about 15-20 minutes shorter. If you substitute a 7 inch/18 cm tin – having first checked that the mixture will fit into it – it will take 15-20 minutes longer cooking time because of the greater depth. Check that the cake does not overbrown during this time: you may need to reduce the heat.

* Test the cake or bread carefully before assuming it is cooked. Advice on how to do this is given in the recipes.

Freezing Teatime Food

Most cakes, breads and scones freeze well, so do sandwiches, unless the filling includes salad ingredients, cooked eggs and a generous amount of mayonnaise. Rich fruit cakes are better stored in an airtight tin to mature. Biscuits keep well in airtight tins.

If you slice large cakes and loaves before freezing you can take out the required number of portions without defrosting the whole cake or loaf. Cakes topped with cream or icing or of a delicate texture should be frozen on an open tray. When quite hard pack or wrap. Remove from the wrapping before defrosting. Glacé icing on a cake does not freeze as well as butter icing.

Modern Yeast Cookery

There are a number of recipes using yeast in this book, as it has been an important ingredient in British cookery for centuries. I give fresh (compressed) yeast in the recipes. This is quite easy to obtain; it keeps for 6-7 days in the refrigerator if it is well wrapped and stored in a screw-topped jar. It should be pale putty-coloured, smell pleasant and crumble readily.

You can freeze fresh yeast for up to 3 months; cut it into convenient sized portions, wrap them well and then freeze.

Dried (active dry) yeast is an excellent alternative. It keeps for a long period; see the packet for details. In place of 1 oz/25 g (1 cake) of fresh yeast use 1/2 oz/15 g (2 teaspoons) of dried yeast. Dissolve 1 teaspoon of sugar in the warm liquid before adding the yeast; wait for 10 minutes, blend well and continue as for fresh yeast.

There are various forms of dried yeast. The 'Easy-Blend' type means you can add the yeast to the flour. 'Fast Acting' means you can cut down on the time required for proving (rising). Follow the packet instructions carefully.

To Follow the Recipes

The recipes in this book are given in Imperial, metric and American measures. The American measures are in brackets. Always follow just one set of measures. In some recipes you will find a slight deviation from the standard metric weights. For example, 3 oz is generally 75 g but occasionally it is given as 85 g, and 4 oz as 110 g instead of 100 g. The reason is to preserve the correct balance with other ingredients in the recipe. If your scales do not register 85 g or 110 g do not worry but remember to be slightly generous with that ingredient.

Spoon measures should be level. Sometimes you will find the word 'level' inserted. This is to stress that the cake, or other dish, could be spoiled if you are over-generous with that ingredient.

I have not given the metric equivalent of teaspoons or tablespoons in the recipes. You may like to know that an American or British teaspoon is equivalent to a 5 ml spoon, a British tablespoon equivalent to a 15 ml spoon. One British tablespoon equals 1 1/4 American tablespoons. American tablespoon measures are expressed in brackets as (tbsp).

Egg sizes are given only where the size of egg used will affect the end result.

Teatime for Slimmers

The key to successful slimming is to have well-balanced, low-calorie and enjoyable meals. This will help you avoid the feeling of hunger which so often makes people forsake their diet and seek a quick snack, which may be high in calories. The longest gap seems to be the one between lunch and the evening meal, but this can be broken by having a light and well-chosen teatime meal.

Tea is an ideal beverage for anyone on a slimming diet, because it is virtually calorie-free. You can have tea with lemon or with skimmed milk or by itself. Make teatime last as long as you can; sip the tea and eat the food slowly: this often makes one feel the meal is larger and more satisfying than it really is.

Sandwiches

Cut thin slices of bread. A slice of bread from a small loaf weighing 1 oz/25 g has about 70 calories.

Spread the bread thinly with butter, margarine or special low-fat spread, then sandwich the slices together with a generous amount of salad ingredients, such as tomatoes, lettuce, cucumber, watercress or grated carrot. Season with a little sea salt, ground black pepper and lemon juice.

Blend low-fat cottage or ricotta cheese with chopped herbs for a savoury filling or with a little dried fruit for something sweeter.

Crispbreads are low in calories and can be used as the base for open sandwiches.

Scones and Cakes

Plain scones or Scotch Pancakes (see pages 86-87) are perfect for tea. If they are really fresh, you need very little butter or margarine or low-fat spread. An average scone has about 90 calories; a Scotch Pancake, weighing 1 oz/25 g has approximately 75 calories.

As most cakes contain a generous amount of fat and sugar they are high in calories. The Sponge Cake on page 103 is a good choice for slimmers, since a 1 oz/25 g portion has about 75 calories. The same weight of the Dundee Cake on page 90 has 120 calories.

Most practical slimming diets suggest you give yourself an occasional 'treat', and what better time to indulge yourself than teatime.

Regency Teatime

The Regency period extended from 1811 to 1820, when the Prince of Wales, who later became King George IV, assumed the powers of regent during the illnesses of his father, George III. The Prince Regent loved a carefree life. At this sociable period in history, tea gardens, described on page 12, were immensely popular; many people were well acquainted with the delights of taking tea. Public social gatherings, known as assemblies, as well as grand balls, were an essential part of fashionable life in London, Bath and Brighton.

The word 'rout' was used to describe a fashionable gathering or assembly of the kind that was much in vogue in the eighteenth and early nineteenth centuries, and gave its name to the small cakes and biscuits (cookies) on the opposite page. It is quite likely that rout cakes would be offered when people returned home, late at night, almost certainly with a cup of tea.

The credit for establishing afternoon tea as an event belongs to Anna, wife of the seventh Duke of Bedford, who lived from 1788 to 1861. She filled the gap between luncheon and evening dinner with tea and light refreshments because 'she had a sinking feeling'. There is no doubt that other fashionable ladies would have followed her excellent example. Madeira cake may well have appeared on the Duchess's tea table, and may also have been offered to mid-morning callers with a glass of Madeira wine.

'Thank Heaven I was not born before the coming-in of tea!'

Reverend Sydney Smith (1771-1845)

Rout Cakes

These are like Ratafias (see page 63) but the mixture is bound with
the yolk of an egg, not the white.
The nut topping makes the biscuits beautifully crisp.

Lightly grease 3 flat baking (cookie) sheets or trays. Heat the oven to 375-400F/190-200C/Gas Mark 5 or 6. Choose the lower setting if your oven cooks quickly.

Blend all the ingredients together in a mixing bowl and form into very small balls. If sticky use damp fingers or chill the mixture for a short time. Put the balls on the prepared sheets or trays and carefully press a few chopped almonds into the top of each one. Brush the nuts with whisked egg white. Place the trays in the oven and bake for 5-6 minutes only. The nuts should be crisp and the biscuits firm on the outside but moist in the centre.

To Make a Change
Rout Biscuits. Cream 4 oz/100 g (1/2 cup) butter with 4 oz/110 g (1/2 cup) caster (granulated) sugar and 1/2 teaspoon of orange flower water or rose water. Beat in 1 egg yolk. Add 8 oz/225 g (2 cups) plain (all-purpose) flour and 4 oz/110 g (2/3 cup) currants.

Knead the mixture well. Roll out on a floured surface until about 1/4 inch/6 mm in thickness. Cut into small fancy shapes. Put on to ungreased baking (cookie) sheets and bake for 15 minutes in preheated moderate oven, 350F/180C/Gas Mark 4. Store in an airtight tin.

Makes up to 60

4 oz/110 g (1 cup) ground almonds

4 oz/110 g (1/2 cup) caster (granulated) sugar

a few drops of almond or ratafia essence (extract)

1 egg yolk

For the topping

approximately 2 oz/50 g (1/2 cup) almonds, blanched and finely chopped

1 egg white, lightly whisked

Georgian Bread

This recipe gives an idea of the flavour of bread in the Regency period,
when the flour that was termed 'white' was certainly not the white flour we know today.
The dough was generally formed into a large round
about 1 inch/2.5 cm thick, but you can make a different shape if you wish.

Makes 1 loaf

1/2 oz/15 g (1/2 cake) fresh (compressed) yeast (for time-saving yeasts, see page 50)

1/4 pint/150 ml (2/3 cup) brown ale

1/4 pint/150 ml (2/3 cup) water

2 teaspoons clear honey

12 oz/350 g (3 cups) brown strong (hard wheat) flour or plain (all-purpose) flour

4 oz/110 g (1 cup) white strong (hard wheat) flour or plain (all-purpose) flour

1/2 teaspoon salt

First cream the yeast. Warm the ale and water to blood heat. Add the honey and stir to dissolve. Carefully mix this liquid with the yeast in a bowl. Sprinkle a little of the flour on top and put in a warm place for about 10 minutes or until the surface is covered with bubbles.

Sift the brown and white flours with salt into a mixing bowl. Add the yeast liquid and blend well. You should have a soft dough, but one that can be kneaded quite easily. If it is too dry, add a very little more warm water. Flours vary, even today, in the amount of liquid they absorb. Knead the dough until it is smooth. It is sufficiently kneaded when the dough springs back when pressed with a floured finger. Return the dough to the bowl. Cover and leave at room temperature for approximately 1 1/2 hours, or until it has risen to nearly twice its original size. Knead again then form into the desired shape.

Place the dough on a warmed baking (cookie) sheet or tray. Cover with lightly oiled polythene and leave for 25-30 minutes until it has nearly doubled in size. Meanwhile heat the oven to 425F/220C/Gas Mark 7. Place the tray in the oven and bake for approximately 30 minutes. To test if cooked, tap the loaf on the bottom, it should sound hollow.

Madeira Cake

Traditionally offered to mid-morning callers with a glass of Madeira,
this cake soon became a teatime favourite as well.

Grease and flour, or line, a 7 inch/18 cm round cake tin (pan). Heat the oven to 325F/160C/Gas Mark 3.

Cream the butter, sugar and lemon rind together until soft and light. The higher amount of sugar gives a sweeter taste and helps to produce a very light-textured cake. Gradually beat in the eggs, adding a little of the flour if necessary to prevent the mixture separating.

Fold in the plain flour and baking powder or the self-raising flour. If you use plain flour and baking powder the cake will be flatter on top. Spoon the mixture into the prepared tin.

Place in the centre of the oven and bake for approximately $1\frac{1}{4}$-$1\frac{1}{2}$ hours. After 30 minutes' cooking time, open the oven door and place the peel on top of the cake (do not remove the cake from the oven). If the cake seems to be getting too brown, lower the heat slightly.

If preferred, the lemon peel can be put on the cake before baking and covered halfway through the cooking period with a piece of foil to prevent it becoming dry or burned. Test the cake by pressing firmly on top. Turn the cake out carefully and leave to cool on a wire tray.

To Make a Change
The flavour and texture of this Madeira Cake are enhanced if 2 oz/50 g ($\frac{1}{2}$ cup) ground almonds are substituted for the same weight of flour. Sift the baking powder with 6 oz/175 g ($1\frac{1}{2}$ cups) plain (all-purpose) flour and add the ground almonds.

Serves 6-8

6 oz/175 g ($\frac{3}{4}$ cup) butter

6-7 oz/175-200 g ($\frac{3}{4}$-$\frac{7}{8}$ cup) caster (granulated) sugar

1 teaspoon finely grated lemon rind, optional

4 eggs, size 1 or 2 (jumbo)

8 oz/225 g (2 cups) plain (all-purpose) flour sifted with $1\frac{1}{2}$ teaspoons baking powder or self-raising flour

1 large thin slice candied lemon peel

Almond Gingerbread

In the old days ginger bread, as it was called – since it was served as bread,
not as cake – was gilded with gold leaf for special occasions.
From this custom came the expression 'gilding the gingerbread'.

Serves 6-8

7 oz/200 g (1³/₄ cups) plain (all-purpose) flour

1 level teaspoon bicarbonate of soda (baking soda)

1 teaspoon ground ginger

1 oz/25 g (¹/₄ cup) ground almonds

2 oz/50 g (¹/₃ cup) blanched chopped almonds

3 oz/85 g (³/₈ cup) butter or margarine

3 oz/85 g (³/₈ cup) brown sugar

3 oz/85 g (¹/₄ cup) golden (light corn) syrup

1 egg

5 tablespoons (6 tbsp) milk

Line a 7 inch/18 cm square cake tin (pan) with greased greaseproof (wax) paper. Heat the oven to 325F/160C/Gas Mark 3.

Sift the flour, bicarbonate of soda and ground ginger into a mixing bowl. Add the ground almonds and blanched chopped almonds.

Place the butter or margarine, sugar and syrup into a heavy saucepan over a moderate heat, stirring until the ingredients have melted. Pour this liquid over the flour mixture and stir briskly. Beat in the egg. Pour the milk into the saucepan, stirring over a gentle heat to incorporate all the remaining syrup mixture. Add to the mixture in the bowl and beat.

Pour the mixture into the prepared tin. Bake for 55 minutes to 1 hour, or until the gingerbread is firm to a gentle touch. Leave to cool in the tin. When cold, the gingerbread can be iced with glacé icing (see page 105) and topped with blanched and browned almonds.

To Make a Change

Fruit Gingerbread. Add 4 oz/100 g (²/₃ cup) mixed dried fruit or chopped dates to the ingredients above. Bake in the same way as Almond Gingerbread.

Oatie Gingerbread. Omit the ground and chopped almonds from the main recipe. Decrease the amount of flour to 6 oz/175 g (1¹/₂ cups) and add 2 oz/50 g (¹/₃ cup) fairly coarse oatmeal. If you wish, substitute black treacle (molasses) for the syrup to give a dark gingerbread. Bake as Almond Gingerbread.

Victorian Teatime

Afternoon tea originated in the Regency period among fashionable households. In the Victorian era that followed, it became popular in most British homes. Genteel ladies would invite their friends and acquaintances to take tea at their 'At Home'. In the country, fruit cakes and various breads had long been served at the end of a working day at a high tea for farmers and their more prosperous employees. This was also the period when the delightful 'nursery tea' first made its appearance.

A good Victorian tea table would be an impressive sight, groaning under the weight of food. The meal would start with an assortment of delicate sandwiches. The sandwich (attributed to Lord Sandwich, so keen to stay at the gambling table he invented something he could eat without leaving it) was first known in 1780, so that by the time Queen Victoria ascended to the throne in 1837 sandwiches had become quite commonplace. For a polite afternoon tea, sandwiches were necessarily small. Watercress and various homemade potted foods would be used as fillings. In summertime you would undoubtedly be offered cucumber sandwiches. These would be followed by fragile, wafer-thin slices of bread and butter, scones and homemade preserves. The cakes may well have been arranged on 3-tier cake stands and the tea poured from exquisite china or silver teapots.

'Tea cleared my head and left me with no misapprehensions.'

Duke of Wellington (1769-1852)

Victoria Sandwich

This light cake was a favourite with Queen Victoria.
It is sometimes known as a 'Butter Sponge'. The traditional method of calculating
the amount of fat, sugar and flour was to weigh them against the eggs.

Serves 6

6 oz/175 g ($^3/_4$ cup) butter
or margarine

6 oz/175 g ($^3/_4$ cup) caster
(granulated) sugar

3 eggs, size 1 or 2 (jumbo)

6 oz/175 g (1 $^1/_2$ cups) self-
raising flour or plain (all-
purpose) flour sifted with
1 $^1/_2$ teaspoons baking
powder

For the Filling

jam (jelly) or lemon curd

For the topping

caster (granulated) or icing
(confectioners') sugar, sifted

Grease and flour or line two 7$^1/_2$-8 inch/19-20 cm sandwich tins (layer pans). Heat the oven to 350F/180C/Gas Mark 4. If your oven is very gentle use 375F/190C/Gas Mark 5.

Cream the butter or margarine and sugar until soft and light. Beat in the eggs one by one, adding 1 tablespoon flour with each. Fold in the remaining flour and the baking powder, if used. Spoon the mixture into the prepared tins and smooth the tops. Bake for 18-20 minutes, or until no impression is left when you press the centre of the sponges gently but firmly.

Allow to cool for 1 or 2 minutes in the tins. Place a folded teacloth on the palm of one hand and turn one sponge layer out on to it. Invert the layer on to a wire tray, top side uppermost. Repeat with the second layer. When cool, sandwich the layers with jam or lemon curd. Dredge the top with sugar.

The Modern Touch

All-in-One Sponge. Substitute soft margarine, preferably polyunsaturated, for the butter. Put all the ingredients into a mixing bowl and cream for 2 minutes or process for 1 minute in an electric mixer or 30 seconds in a food processor. Bake as above. To counteract the fact that the mixture is not aerated as well as when using the traditional method of creaming, you may like to sift 1 level teaspoon baking powder into the self-raising flour or 1 extra level teaspoon into plain flour.

Battenburg Cake

This is sometimes called a 'Church Window' cake, for the two-coloured squares of sponge with the marzipan coating resemble stained glass.

Line an oblong cake tin (pan) measuring 10 x 7 inches/25 x 18 cm with greased greaseproof (wax) paper, making a pleat in the centre of the paper that stands up in the centre, dividing the tin lengthwise in half. This will separate the two different coloured cake mixtures. Heat the oven to 350F/180C/Gas Mark 4.

Prepare the Victoria Sandwich mixture. Spoon half into one side of the tin. Add a little food colouring to the remaining mixture and spoon this into the other side of the tin. Place in the oven and bake for 30 minutes, or until firm to the touch. Turn out on to a wire tray to cool. Meanwhile make the marzipan by blending together all the ingredients.

Cut each piece of cake lengthwise in half to give 4 strips. Arrange the strips with a coloured and a plain one side by side. Top the plain strip with a coloured one and the coloured one with a plain strip. Join all these together with jam.

Roll out the marzipan on a sugared board to a size that will completely enclose the sponge cake, except for the short ends. Brush all round the cake, but not these ends, with jam. Place the cake in the centre of the marzipan, wrap it around the cake and seal the edges. Turn the cake so the join is underneath. Neaten the ends with a sharp knife. Flute the 4 top edges of the marzipan with finger and thumb. Arrange the cherries and angelica decoratively on top.

Serves 8-10

1 quantity of Victoria Sandwich cake mixture (see opposite)

a few drops of pink food colouring

For the marzipan

8 oz/225 g (2 cups) ground almonds

4 oz/110 g ($1/2$ cup) caster (granulated) sugar

4 oz/110 g (1 cup) icing (confectioners') sugar, well sifted

2 egg yolks

few drops almond essence (extract), optional

For the coating and decoration

6 tablespoons ($1/2$ cup) sieved apricot jam (jelly)

a few glacé (candied) cherries, halved

1 small piece of angelica, cut into leaf shapes

Swiss Roll

This light sponge has been one of the most popular cakes in Britain for many years.
Both the sponge mixture and the filling can be varied as shown opposite.
It can become a truly modern roulade too.
The addition of butter makes a moister sponge that keeps a little longer.
Plain flour is used as the mixture is aerated by whisking
the eggs and sugar, but if you have not made a whisked sponge before,
you could use self-raising flour to ensure the mixture rises.

Serves 6

3 oz/85 g ($^3/_4$ cup) plain (all-
purpose) or self-raising flour

3 eggs, size 1 or 2 (jumbo)

4 oz/110 g ($^1/_2$ cup) caster
(granulated) sugar

1 oz/25 g (2 tbsp) butter,
melted, optional

1 tablespoon (1 $^1/_4$ tbsp) hot
water, optional

For rolling and filling

a little extra caster (granulated)
sugar

jam (jelly)

Line a 12 x 8-9 inch/30.5 x 20-23 cm Swiss roll tin (jelly roll pan) with greased greaseproof (wax) paper or non-stick silicone paper. Heat the oven to 375F/190C/Gas Mark 5.

Sift the flour on to a plate and keep it warm. Put the eggs and sugar into a mixing bowl or the bowl of an electric mixer. Whisk until thick and creamy and the whisk leaves a trail when lifted.

Sift the flour into the egg mixture, then carefully fold in with the butter, if used. The mixture should be of a pouring consistency. If it is slightly stiff, add the water. Spoon or pour into the prepared tin, making sure the corners are filled. Bake towards the top of the oven for about 9 minutes or until firm to a gentle touch.

Meanwhile warm, but do not overheat, the jam. Place a sheet of greaseproof paper on a working surface and sprinkle with caster sugar. Invert the tin over the sugared paper with the short end towards you. Remove the tin and peel off the cooking paper. If it sticks to the sponge, damp the paper with a brush dipped in cold water. If the edges of the sponge are crisp, cut these away. Immediately spread the sponge with the warm jam. Make a light cut across the sponge about $^1/_2$ inch/1.5 cm from the short end nearest to you then make a firm fold.

Using the sugared paper, firmly roll up the sponge. Place the roll on a wire tray to cool completely in a draught-free place.

More Swiss Rolls

The Swiss Roll recipe given opposite can be varied in many ways,
simply by changing
the filling or the flavour of the sponge mixture.

Cream-filled Swiss Rolls

Turn the sponge out on to the sugared paper and roll it up immediately with the paper in between the layers, so they do not stick together. When it is cold, carefully unroll the sponge. Spread with warm jam, redcurrant jelly or a sweetened fruit purée, such as raspberry, then top with 1/4 pint/150 ml (2/3 cup) whipped cream. The cream can be flavoured with a little vanilla sugar or essence (extract) or with a little liqueur.

Here are two particularly delicious fillings.

Black Cherry. Drain cooked or canned black cherries; or remove the stones from really ripe fruit. Soak in a little cherry brandy; do not use any more than the fruit can absorb.

Spread the sponge with a little melted redcurrant jelly then with whipped cream. Add the cherry mixture and re-roll. Decorate with a few whirls of whipped cream and cherries.

Chocolate and Rum. Make a plain or chocolate-flavoured Swiss roll. Whip about 1/4 pint/150 ml (2/3 cup) of double (heavy) cream. Add a little sugar, some grated or finely chopped chocolate and a dash of rum. Spread the sponge with sieved apricot jam (jelly), add the cream mixture and re-roll. The completed roll can be decorated with whirls of whipped cream and chocolate leaves.

Flavouring the Sponge Mixture

Chocolate Sponge. Replace 1/2 oz/15 g (2 tbsp) flour with cocoa powder (unsweetened cocoa), or replace 1 oz/25 g (4 tbsp) flour with sweetened chocolate powder.

Nut Roulade. While you can replace the flour with the same weight of finely chopped nuts, it is easier to use the following combination: 1 1/2 oz/40 g (6 tbsp) flour and 2 oz/50 g (1/2 cup) finely chopped hazelnuts (filberts), pecan nuts or walnuts.

Prepare, cook and fill the sponge as in the basic recipe.

Cherry Cake

The secret of a rich cherry cake, where the cherries stay in position,
is to use a relatively small amount of baking powder and to bake the cake slowly.
If you do this it is unnecessary to wash the cherries.
Do not be disappointed if the cake does not rise very dramatically; the cherries
are heavy and very little raising agent is used.
If you want a deeper cake, use the 7 inch/18 cm tin (pan).

Serves 8

6 oz/175 g ($^3/_4$ cup) butter or margarine

6 oz/175 g ($^3/_4$ cup) caster (granulated) sugar

3 eggs, size 1 or 2 (jumbo) or 4 smaller eggs

8 oz/225 g (2 cups) plain (all-purpose) flour, sifted with 1 teaspoon baking powder

6 oz/175 g ($^3/_4$ cup) glacé (candied) cherries, halved

Grease and lightly flour or line a 7 or 8 inch/18 or 20 cm round cake tin (pan). Heat the oven to 300F/150C/Gas Mark 2.

Cream the butter or margarine and sugar until soft and light. Gradually beat in the eggs. Mix the flour and baking powder with the halved cherries. Fold gently, but thoroughly, into the creamed mixture. Do not add any extra liquid.

Spoon the mixture into the prepared cake tin and smooth it flat on top. Bake in the centre of the oven. The 7 inch/18 cm cake will take approximately 1$^3/_4$ hours and the 8 inch/20 cm cake about 1$^1/_2$ hours. Allow the cake to cool in the tin for 5 minutes then turn out to cool completely on a wire tray.

To Make a Change

Cherry and Almond Cake. Replace 2 oz/50 g ($^1/_2$ cup) of the plain (all-purpose) flour with 3 oz/75 g ($^3/_4$ cup) ground almonds. Do not add almond essence, for the flavour of the ground almonds should be subtle. Put the cake mixture in the prepared tin then top with about 2 oz/50 g ($^1/_2$ cup) blanched and flaked almonds. Bake as above.

Almond Macaroons

Almonds have been used in cooking for centuries.
The Victorian cook would skin, chop and pound the nuts to make ground
almonds – a laborious process.

Line two baking (cookie) sheets or trays with rice paper. Heat the oven to 350F/180C/Gas Mark 4.

Whisk the egg whites until just frothy. Add the almond essence, ground almonds and sugar. If slightly soft, add the rice flour, cornflour or more ground almonds. Form the mixture into 12-18 soft balls and place them on the rice paper, spaced well apart. Top each ball with a blanched almond.

To produce sticky macaroons, put a bowl of water in the oven under the biscuits as they bake. Bake in the centre of the oven for approximately 20 minutes. When they are cool enough to handle, cut round the rice paper.

To Make a Change

Almond Paste Tartlets. Use only 1¹/2 egg whites to make a stiffer mixture. Roll out until very thin on a sugared surface. Cut into 15-18 rounds to fit small patty tins (pans). Bake for 10 minutes at 325F/160C/Gas Mark 3. Cool slightly then lift from the tins. When cold fill with homemade conserve (jelly).

Ratafias. Ratafia essence is extracted from the kernels of cherries, apricots or peaches. Follow the recipe for Macaroons, but roll the mixture into 60-70 small balls and reduce the cooking time to 10 minutes.

Makes 12-18

rice paper

2 egg whites

a few drops of almond or ratafia essence (extract)

5 oz/150 g (1³/4 cups) ground almonds

6 oz/175 g (³/4 cup) caster (granulated) sugar

1 teaspoon rice flour or cornflour (cornstarch), optional

To decorate

12-18 blanched almonds

Meringues

Meringues could be made fairly readily from the beginning of the eighteenth
century, when sugar was more widely available.
When sandwiched together with cream they were known as 'kisses'.
Do not use egg whites that are less than 24 hours old;
very fresh or cold egg whites do not whisk well. If stored in the refrigerator leave to stand at room
temperature for 1 hour. Cover left-over egg yolks with cold water
to prevent a skin from forming, and use for mixing pastry or in baked custards.
While caster sugar is given in the ingredients,
you can use half caster and half sifted icing (confectioners') sugar
or substitute light brown sugar for the caster sugar.

Makes 12 large shells
  or 6 'kisses'

2 egg whites

a few drops of vanilla essence
  (extract)

4 oz/110 g (1/2 cup) caster
  (granulated) sugar

For the filling

1/4 pint/150 ml (2/3 cup)
  double (heavy) cream,
  whipped

Prepare the baking (cookie) trays well; meringues are inclined to stick. Use non-stick silicone paper or silicone-coated trays or, if using ordinary tins (pans), brush them lightly with olive oil, or a few drops of melted butter, or line with oiled or greased greaseproof (wax) paper. Heat the oven to 200-225F/90-110C/Gas Mark 0 or 1/4 or S. If you prefer to cook the meringues slightly faster, so they are softer in the middle, use 225-250F/110-120C/Gas Mark 1/4-1/2.

Whisk the egg whites until stiff but do not overwhip them. Add the vanilla essence. Either, whisk in half the sugar then fold in the remainder or, if using an electric mixer, set it to a low speed and add the sugar steadily.

Fill a spoon with meringue mixture, take a second spoon and scoop out the mixture on to the prepared surface. Use a rolling movement and you will achieve a good shape. Repeat with the remaining mixture. Alternatively, place the mixture in a piping bag fitted with a large star nozzle and pipe 12 meringues in decorative shapes. Dust with a little extra sugar if desired.

Bake for 2-3 hours. They will feel crisp on the outside when adequately cooked. Remove from the sheets with a warmed knife and leave to cool. Store in an airtight tin until required.

To make 'kisses', gently break just the bottom surface of each meringue. Sandwich them together in pairs, bottom to bottom, with whipped cream.

Brandy Snaps

These crisp wafers have been made for centuries. It is believed
they have evolved from the old English wafers known as 'gauffres'.
Originally a teaspoon of brandy would have been added. They can be served plain,
or filled with whipped cream.

Grease 2 or 3 baking (cookie) sheets or trays. Heat the oven to 325F/160C/Gas Mark 3.

Place the butter and sugar with the syrup or honey into a saucepan and heat gently until the butter has melted and the sugar dissolved. This could be done in a basin in a microwave oven. Cool slightly then add the flour, ground ginger and brandy, if used. Mix well.

Put teaspoons of the mixture on to the prepared sheets or trays, allowing space for the mixture to spread. Place the first tray into the oven and bake for 8-12 minutes, or until the edges become firm. In order to allow time to roll the thin biscuits (cookies) it is advisable to bake one batch at a time, so put the second batch into the oven as you remove the first.

Grease the handle of a wooden spoon. Let the brandy snaps cool for 1 or 2 minutes. Remove one with a palette knife and roll it around the spoon handle; hold in position for a few seconds then slip out the handle and place the biscuit on a wire tray with the overlapping edge downwards. Repeat with the remaining biscuits. If they begin to harden on the trays before you can roll them, warm for a short time in the oven.

Store brandy snaps separately in an airtight tin.

Makes 15-16

2 oz/50 g (1/4 cup) butter

2 oz/50 g (1/4 cup) caster (granulated) sugar

2 oz/50 g (3 tbsp) golden (light corn) syrup or honey

2 oz/50 g (1/4 cup) plain (all-purpose) flour

1/2-1 teaspoon ground ginger, optional

1 teaspoon brandy, optional

Teatime in England

Although England is a comparatively small country it has always maintained very strong regional customs and differences, many of which, as in other cultures, are related to food, particularly the kind of food served at that most English of meals, teatime.

In the North of England, for example, you will be offered deliciously light Eccles Cakes (page 82) and Yorkshire's Fat Rascals (page 74) spread with a generous amount of butter.

Devon and Cornwall, in the West Country, are famous for their cream teas. I have given a recipe for real Devonshire Splits on page 71. If you do not have time to make them, choose the recipe for Scones on page 87, but in either case, serve with fruity jam (jelly) and lots of clotted or whipped cream.

Sally Lunns (page 69), a special teacake, are reputed to have originated in the Roman city of Bath, but have now become available in most parts of England, including the North. Similar cakes are known in other countries too.

'Stands the Church clock at ten to three?
And is there honey still for tea?'

The Old Vicarage, Grantchester. Rupert Brooke (1887-1915)

Making Sandwiches

Teatime sandwiches can be made in many attractive shapes. If you are entertaining people who enjoy playing cards then cut the sandwiches in the shape of clubs, diamonds, hearts and spades (special cutters are available). Neat finger shapes are easy to cut if you are in a hurry. It is usual to cut off the crusts for afternoon-tea sandwiches.

Rolled sandwiches look very attractive. Cut large thin slices of fresh bread and spread with butter. Top with a smooth-textured filling, then roll the bread firmly. If the bread is difficult to roll, treat each slice as though it was pastry and roll a rolling pin firmly over the bread before spreading it with the butter and filling. This makes the bread very pliable. To make pinwheel sandwiches, cut the rolls in thin slices.

Open sandwiches look colourful and appetizing. Top fingers or rounds of buttered bread with a small amount of topping; too much can easily fall off.

Keep sandwiches in the refrigerator until you are ready to serve. Cover the plates or dishes or flat trays with foil or cling film (plastic wrap).

Freezing sandwiches. Most sandwiches freeze well, but not those containing salad ingredients, egg or a generous amount of mayonnaise. Freeze on a flat tray then wrap. Unwrap before defrosting.

Sandwich fillings

Based on Cheese
Blend cream or curd cheese with finely chopped dates or nuts, well-drained pineapple, diced cucumber, shredded lettuce or watercress leaves.

Add sufficient mayonnaise to grated cheese to give it a soft consistency.

Based on Eggs
Chop hard-boiled eggs and add enough mayonnaise to make a spreading consistency, spread the buttered bread with lumpfish roe (mock caviar) and top with the egg.

Mix scrambled egg with watercress, or mustard and cress, or finely diced red (sweet) peppers. Flavour scrambled eggs with a pinch of curry powder and chutney.

Based on Fish
Flavour smoked salmon with a squeeze of lemon juice and use as a sandwich filling with crisp lettuce.

Cooked fresh salmon, flaked smoke trout or mackerel all make excellent sandwich fillings. Blend the fish with a little mayonnaise or horseradish cream.

Potted fish (see page 145) is an ideal filling.

Based on Meat

Fill the bread and butter with thinly sliced cooked chicken, ham or tongue. To add extra flavour to the sandwiches add crisp lettuce and blend a small amount of mustard or chutney to the butter used for spreading the bread. Pâtés of all kinds can be used.

Based on Salads

Any of the crisp salad greens can be used as a sandwich filling combined with sliced cucumber, chopped peppers or thinly sliced raw mushrooms blended with a little mayonnaise. Be restrained with sliced tomatoes, too many of which make the bread over-soft.

To make traditional cucumber sandwiches, peel the cucumber, if liked, then slice thinly and place on a plate with a little salt and pepper. Cover and leave for an hour. The excess liquid will run out, leaving the cucumber beautifully firm.

Sally Lunns

*Sally Lunn was famous for the cakes she sold in Bath in the eighteenth century.
It is believed she gave her name to this teacake.
A second theory is that the name comes from the French 'le soleil et la lune'
(the sun and the moon), presumably because they tasted
good any time of day or night. Single cream is believed to have been
used in the original recipe and it makes a very rich teabread,
but milk is quite adequate.*

Sift the flour and salt into a mixing bowl. Cream the yeast in a bowl, warm the cream or milk to blood heat and add it to the yeast. Blend thoroughly. Sprinkle a little flour on top and leave in a warm place for about 10 minutes or until the surface is covered with bubbles.

Rub the butter or margarine into the flour and add the sugar. Make a well in the centre of the mixture and pour in the yeast liquid. Add the eggs and blend thoroughly. The dough should be soft but easy to knead on a floured surface until it is smooth in texture.

Return the dough to a large mixing bowl, cover and leave to 'prove' (rise) until almost doubled in size. This will take approximately 1^1/$_2$ hours at room temperature.

Meanwhile grease three 5 inch/12.5 cm round cake tins (pans) and leave in a warm place. Heat the oven to 450F/230C/Gas Mark 8.

Knead the risen dough again and divide it into three portions. Shape into balls and place in the tins. Cover and leave for 30 minutes or until well risen. Bake for 15-20 minutes. To test the loaves, tap the bottom; they should sound hollow.

Serve with butter or clotted cream.

Makes 3 small loaves

12 oz/350 g (3 cups) strong (hard wheat) flour or plain (all-purpose) flour

a pinch of salt

^{3}/$_4$ oz/20 g (^{3}/$_4$ cake) fresh (compressed) yeast (for time-saving yeasts, see page 50)

^{1}/$_4$ pint/150 ml (^{2}/$_3$ cup) single (light) cream or milk

4 oz/100 g (^{1}/$_2$ cup) butter or margarine

4 oz/100 g (^{1}/$_2$ cup) caster (granulated) sugar

2 eggs

Bath Buns

These are among the richest and most delicious of all yeast cakes.
Do make them at home; sadly the buns that you buy bear no resemblance
to the traditional bun that originated in the city of Bath.
If you cannot obtain loaf sugar use granulated or even demerara sugar.

Makes 12

Ingredients as Sally Lunns (see page 69) plus:

2 eggs

4-6 oz/100-175 g (3/4-1 cup) mixed dried fruit

2-3 oz/50-75 g (1/3-1/2 cup) candied peel, chopped

For the topping

8-10 lumps of loaf sugar, lightly crushed, see method

Follow the directions for making Sally Lunns on page 69, adding the dried fruit and peel to the flour. Knead the dough and allow to prove (rise) in exactly the same way as given in that recipe.

Meanwhile grease 2 or 3 flat baking (cookie) sheets or trays. You need to allow plenty of space between the buns, for the soft dough spreads as well as rises during cooking.

Form the dough into 12 rounds. The traditional bun is fairly large, but you could make smaller ones if preferred. Place on the warm sheets or trays. Press the crushed sugar lightly but firmly on top of the buns. Lightly cover the buns with oiled cling film (plastic wrap); leave in a warm place for 20-25 minutes, or until nearly doubled in size.

Meanwhile heat the oven to 425F/220C/Gas Mark 7. Make sure the oven is really hot before baking. Bake the buns for 15 minutes or until well risen and firm. Smaller buns would take a slightly shorter time. Bath Buns should not be allowed to become too brown in colour – they should be golden.

Devonshire Splits

Both Cornwall and Devon take pride in their traditional teas of splits,
served with clotted cream and jam (jelly).
Nowadays you will often be served light scones (biscuits) for splits
instead of these yeast buns.

Cream the yeast in a bowl then add the water and a sprinkling of flour; leave in a warm place until the surface is covered with bubbles.

Put the flour, salt and sugar into a large bowl; add the yeast liquid and the butter or margarine. Mix together well. Add the egg and knead to make a smooth dough. The mixture will be fairly soft at this stage, but this is as it should be.

Continue kneading the dough until it is smooth. To test for readiness, press the dough with a lightly floured finger; if it leaves an impression, continue kneading. When the dough is ready any impression comes out.

Return the dough to the bowl, cover and leave in a warm place for 1¼-1½ hours, or until nearly doubled in size. Meanwhile, grease and flour 2 or 3 baking (cookie) sheets or trays and leave in a warm place. Turn the risen dough out on to a floured surface and knead until smooth. Divide into about 20 portions.

Form them into rounds like buns or slightly larger and flatter rounds. Fold these in half so that the splits can be broken open, rather than cut. Place on the warmed sheets or trays; cover with lightly oiled cling film (plastic wrap). Leave for 20-30 minutes, or until risen to almost twice the original size.

Meanwhile, heat the oven to 450F/230C/Gas Mark 8. Bake the splits for 10 minutes, or until firm but pale in colour; they should not be too brown.

Serve with bowls of clotted or whipped cream and jam (jelly).

Makes 20

1 oz/25 g (1 cake) fresh (compressed) yeast (for time-saving yeasts, see page 50)

8 fl oz/225 ml (1 cup) warm water

1 lb/450 g (4 cups) strong (hard wheat) flour or plain (all-purpose) flour

a good pinch of salt

2 oz/50 g (¼ cup) caster (granulated) sugar

2 oz/50 g (¼ cup) butter or margarine, melted and allowed to cool

l egg

Muffins

The word 'muffin' is used to describe several kinds of teacake. There are 2 British variations, one not unlike a Scone (see page 87), and the other, which is given below, a traditional yeast recipe cooked on a griddle. The second recipe is for the delicious American version, which are baked in tins, 'puff up' and are very light.

Yeast Muffins

Makes 12

1/2 oz/15 g (1/2 cake) fresh (compressed) yeast (for time-saving yeasts, see page 50)

1/2 pint/300 ml (1 1/4 cups) warm milk

14 oz/400 g (3 1/2 cups) plain (all-purpose) flour

1/2 teaspoon salt

Cream the yeast in a bowl and add the milk. Sprinkle a little flour on top and leave in a warm place for 10 minutes, or until the surface is covered in bubbles.

Sift the flour with the salt into a mixing bowl. Add the yeast liquid and mix well. Knead until a smooth but soft dough is formed. Cover the bowl and leave at room temperature for 1 1/4 hours, or until the dough has doubled in size. Knead it once more, and divide into 12 equal portions.

For a perfect shape you should use 12 muffin rings about 3 inches/7.5 cm in diameter. Place them on to greased trays. Form the dough portions into pieces to fit the rings (if you have no rings simply make dough circles of the same size). The muffins should be fairly thick. Cover lightly and leave for about 25 minutes or until well risen.

Heat a griddle and grease it lightly. Lift the muffins – in their rings if you are using them – on to the griddle. Cook for 4-4 1/2 minutes or until lightly browned on the bottom. Turn and cook the other side in the same way. Serve hot or warm with butter.

American Muffins

This basic recipe can be varied with the addition of fresh fruits
– blueberries are the classic – or dried fruit.
A little of the flour can be replaced by bran. Try savoury muffins,
using seasoning instead of sugar and a little grated cheese. Serve with butter.

Heat the oven to 425F/220C/Gas Mark 7. Grease 12 deep patty tins (pans). Sift the flour and baking powder into a mixing bowl with the salt. Add the sugar, milk, egg and butter and mix well. Spoon into the tins. Place in the oven and bake for 25-30 minutes or until well risen.

Makes 12

8 oz/225 g (2 cups) self-raising flour with 1 teaspoon baking powder or plain (all-purpose) flour with 3 teaspoons baking powder

$^1/_2$ teaspoon salt

2 tablespoons (2 $^1/_2$ tbsp) caster or granulated sugar

8 fl oz/240 ml (1 cup) milk

1 egg

2 tablespoons (2 $^1/_2$ tbsp) melted butter

Fat Rascals

These are a Yorkshire speciality; they are light and slightly sweet scones (biscuits) that are traditionally served with butter.

Makes 10-12

8 oz/225 g (2 cups) self-raising flour or plain (all-purpose) flour sifted with 2 teaspoons baking powder

4 oz/100 g (1/2 cup) butter or margarine

2 oz/50 g (1/4 cup) light brown sugar

2 oz/50 g (1/3 cup) currants

approximately 1/4 pint/150 ml (2/3 cup) milk

milk and a little caster or granulated sugar, to glaze

Dust an ungreased baking (cookie) sheet with a little flour to prevent the bottom of the scones becoming too brown. Heat the oven to 425F/220C/Gas Mark 7.

Rub the butter or margarine into the flour, or flour and baking powder. Add the sugar and currants. Mix with the milk to give a soft rolling consistency. Knead lightly to form a smooth round and place on a lightly floured surface. Roll out until approximately 3/4 inch/2 cm in thickness; cut into rounds or triangles. Brush each Fat Rascal with a little milk to glaze and sprinkle with a little sugar. Place on the prepared sheet and bake towards the top of the oven for 10 minutes, or until firm when pressed on the side. Transfer to a wire tray to cool.

Cornish Saffron Cakes

It is interesting that in Britain we tend to use saffron, which comes from the
stamens of a certain crocus, to flavour cakes,
rather than adding it to savoury dishes, as is done in other countries.
Measure the saffron powder carefully, for it is expensive and thrifty
Cornish cooks would not use too much.

If using saffron strands put them into a cup with 1 tablespoon boiling water and leave to stand until the water is cold. Most people strain the liquid and use it in place of some of the milk, but I have seen the strands left in these small cakes and they are really quite pleasant.

Lightly grease 2 baking (cookie) sheets or trays. Heat the oven to 425F/220C/Gas Mark 7.

Sift the saffron powder with the flour and baking powder if used and the cinnamon. Rub in the butter or margarine. Add the sugar, dried fruit, candied peel, caraway seeds and the egg. Mix very thoroughly. Slowly add just enough milk or saffron water to make a sticky consistency.

Put the mixture into 12 small heaps on the sheets or trays, leaving room for the cakes to spread. Bake for 12-15 minutes or until firm and golden brown on the outside.

Makes 12

1/4 teaspoon saffron powder or 10-12 saffron strands

8 oz/225 g (2 cups) self-raising flour or plain (all-purpose) flour sifted with 2 teaspoons baking powder

a pinch of ground cinnamon, optional

4 oz/110 g (1/4 cup) butter or margarine

4 oz/110 g (1/4 cup) caster (granulated) sugar

2 oz/50 g (1/3 cup) currants

2 oz/50 g (1/3 cup) seedless raisins

2 oz/50 g (1/3 cup) candied peel, finely chopped

1/2 teaspoon caraway seeds

l egg

a little milk, to mix

Raisin and Orange Cake

This is based on the type of eggless fruit cake that was such a standby during the years of rationing in Britain. It is ideal for people who are allergic to eggs.

Serves 6-8

10 oz/300 g (2 1/2 cups) self-raising flour or plain (all-purpose) flour sifted with 2 1/2 teaspoons baking powder

1/2 teaspoon bicarbonate of soda (baking soda)

7 fl oz/200 ml (generous 3/4 cup) moderately strong blended or Darjeeling tea, well strained

2 teaspoons grated orange rind

3 oz/85 g (3/8 cup) butter or margarine

4 oz/100 g (scant 1/2 cup) brown sugar

1 tablespoon (1 1/4 tbsp) orange marmalade

4 oz/100 g (2/3 cup) seedless raisins

1 oz/25 g (3 tbsp) candied orange peel, finely chopped

Line an 8 inch/20 cm round cake tin (pan) with greased greaseproof (wax) paper. Heat the oven to 350F/180C/Gas Mark 4.

Sift the dry ingredients together. Pour the tea into a large saucepan and add the orange rind, butter or margarine, sugar and marmalade. Heat until the butter and sugar have melted then add the dried fruit. Boil the mixture for 1 minute only. Add the candied peel and leave to become quite cold. Pour the tea mixture over the dry ingredients and beat well. Spoon into the prepared tin and smooth flat on top. Bake for 1 1/4 hours or until firm to the touch. Check after 55 minutes and reduce the heat slightly if the cake is becoming too brown.

The Modern Touch

It is important to include plenty of fibre in the diet. This cake is extremely pleasant if made with wholemeal (wholewheat) flour in place of white flour. There is no need to increase the liquid content.

Somerset Apple Cake

Most of the counties of southern and south-west England have their traditional recipes for apple cakes. This is one of the simplest and nicest.
The secret is to use really good cooking (baking) apples.

Line the base of an 8 inch/20 cm round or 7 inch/18 cm square cake tin (pan); grease and flour the sides.

Heat the oven to 350F/180C/Gas Mark 4.

Cut the peeled and cored apples into neat 1/2 inch/1.5 cm dice and combine with 1 oz/25 g (2 tbsp) of the sugar and the ground cinnamon. Rub the butter or margarine into the flour and baking powder, if used, until the mixture is like fine breadcrumbs. Add the remaining sugar, then the apples. Mix together thoroughly. Add the egg and milk and stir briskly. The dough may appear a little stiff and crumbly at first but it very quickly binds together. Spoon into the prepared tin and sprinkle demerara sugar on top.

Bake in the oven for 1 1/4 hours. If the cake is becoming a little too brown on top reduce the heat after 1 hour. Allow to cool for 5-10 minutes in the cake tin, then turn out carefully on to a wire tray.

Like most apple cakes, this is nicest served very fresh and even slightly warm.

Serves 8

2 medium cooking (baking) apples yielding 8 oz/225 g (2 cups) when peeled and cored

6 oz/175 g (scant 3/4 cup) demerara sugar

1/2 teaspoon ground cinnamon, or to taste

5 oz/150 g (5/8 cup) butter or margarine

8 oz/225 g (2 cups) self-raising flour or plain (all-purpose) flour sifted with 2 teaspoons baking powder

l egg

1 tablespoon (1 1/4 tbsp) milk

For the topping

2 tablespoons (2 1/2 tbsp) demerara sugar (light brown)

Madeleines

The cakes well known to the French as 'Madeleines' are plain and fairly flat in shape.
The English version, given here, is a castle shape,
coated with jam and coconut. The tall pudding tins (pans) in which they are baked
are called dariole moulds.

Makes 12-16

4 oz/110 g (1/2 cup) butter or
margarine

4 oz/110 g (1/2 cup) caster
(granulated) sugar

2 eggs, size 1 or 2 (jumbo)

4 oz/110 g (1 cup) self-raising
flour or plain (all-purpose)
flour sifted with 1 teaspoon
baking powder

For the coating and decoration

approximately 4 tablespoons (5
tbsp) raspberry or apricot jam
(jelly), sieved

2 oz/50 g (2/3 cup) desiccated
(shredded) coconut

6-8 glacé (candied) cherries,
halved

a small piece of angelica, cut
into leaf shapes

Grease and flour 12 large or 16 smaller dariole moulds. Heat the oven
to 400F/200C/Gas Mark 6.

Cream the butter or margarine and sugar until soft and light.
Gradually beat in the eggs, then fold in the flour, or flour and baking
powder. Spoon the mixture into the prepared moulds. It is important
that they are only just over half filled, for the cakes should not rise
above the top of the tins during baking. Tap each mould lightly on the
work surface to make sure they are filled at the base.

Place the moulds on a flat baking (cookie) sheet or tray. Place in the
oven towards the top, and bake for 10 minutes, or until firm to the
touch. Cool for a minute then turn out carefully on to a wire tray to
cool.

Warm the jam slightly and spread the coconut out on a flat plate.
Brush or spread the jam over the top and sides of the cakes then roll
them in the coconut until evenly coated. You will find this easier to do
if you insert a fine skewer in the base of the cake and hold this. Top
each cake with a halved cherry and leaves of angelica.

Puff Pastry

The proportions used below are correct for puff pastry, but the method is that generally used to make rough puff, which is a little easier.
The pastry does not rise quite as dramatically as when the classic method is used, but it is ideal for the recipes in this book.
This quantity is equivalent to 12 oz/350 g (3/4 lb) commercially frozen puff pastry.

Cut the butter, which should be at room temperature, into 3/4 inch/2 cm pieces. Sift the flour and salt into a mixing bowl. Add the butter, turning it in the flour to coat the pieces. Mix the lemon juice and water. Stir it into the flour, blending together with a palette knife (spatula). Do not break the pieces of fat. The amount of liquid given should be sufficient to make a pliable dough. Flours vary slightly in the amount of liquid they absorb, so add a little more water if necessary. Form the dough into a neat shape.

Flour a pastry board and rolling pin. Roll the dough to make an oblong 3 times longer than its width.

Bring the bottom third of the dough over the middle third, giving the effect of an opened envelope. Bring down the top third, thus closing the 'envelope'. Turn the dough 90 degrees so you have an open end towards you. Seal both open ends with the rolling pin and depress the pastry dough with the pin at regular intervals: this is known as 'ribbing' it.

Roll out the dough with short sharp light movements to re-form an oblong. Fold as before, turn the pastry, seal the ends and 'rib' the pastry. Cover and chill for about 30 minutes. Do not let it become too hard.

Repeat the process of rolling, folding and ribbing 3 times more. Chill the pastry before using, completely covered so that a skin does not form.

The Modern Touch

Homemade puff pastry can be successfully frozen. Make a large batch and divide it into neat portions. Cover lightly, freeze until firm then wrap.

6 oz/175 g (3/4 cup) butter

6 oz/175 g (1 1/2 cups) strong (hard wheat) or plain (all-purpose) flour

a pinch of salt

1 teaspoon lemon juice

about 6 tablespoons (1/2 cup) ice-cold water

Maids of Honour

Some sources say that these famous cakes were prepared by the ill-fated Anne Boleyn (mother of Elizabeth I) to please Henry VIII.
Others say they were made for Anne by her own maids of honour.

Makes 12-15

1 quantity Puff Pastry (see page 79)

For the filling

6 oz/175 g (^{3}/4 cup) cottage cheese, sieved

2 oz/50 g (^{1}/4 cup) butter

2 oz/50 g (^{1}/4 cup) caster (granulated) sugar

1 oz/25 g (^{1}/4 cup) ground almonds

2 egg yolks

2 teaspoons brandy

^{1}/2 teaspoon grated lemon rind

2 tablespoons (2^1/2 tbsp) currants

Roll out the pastry and cut it into rounds; line 12-15 deep patty tins (pans). Chill well while preparing the filling. Heat the oven to 425F/220C/Gas Mark 7.

Blend all the ingredients, except the currants, together. Spoon the mixture into the pastry cases and sprinkle the currants over the filling. Bake for 10 minutes in the hot oven, then reduce the heat to 325F/160C/Gas Mark 3 for a further 15 minutes, or until both filling and pastry are firm.

To Make a Change

Sometimes Maids of Honour are topped with a round of glacé icing. Blend 4 oz/100 g (1 cup) sifted icing (confectioners') sugar with a few drops of lemon juice and enough cold water to make a spreading consistency. Spoon a wafer-thin layer on the tarts. Decorate with glacé cherries and angelica.

Almond Maids of Honour. This filling is firmer, but equally delicious, and also attributed to Anne Boleyn. Whisk 1 egg and 1 egg yolk with 2 oz/50 g (^{1}/4 cup) caster (granulated) sugar until thick. Add 1 teaspoon of orange flower water, 1 teaspoon brandy, 4 oz/100 g (1 cup) ground almonds and 1 oz/25 g (^{1}/4 cup) fine cake crumbs. Mix well. Put into the pastry cases and bake as above. These can be iced if desired, as above.

Cherry Tartlets

These small fruit tartlets are ideal for teatime in hot weather.
It is a good idea to bake a large batch of tartlet cases and keep these in the freezer.
Small strawberries can be used instead of cherries for the filling.

Sift the flour and cornflour into a bowl; rub in the butter or margarine until the mixture is like fine breadcrumbs. Add the sugar. Make a well in the centre of the mixture, drop in the egg yolk and blend the ingredients together with a palette knife (spatula). Gradually add sufficient water to make a rolling consistency. If the mixture is a little soft wrap it and chill for an hour in the refrigerator.

Knead the dough lightly (this pastry can be handled more than a shortcrust pastry). Roll out on a lightly floured board until 1/4 inch/6 mm in thickness, then cut into rounds to fit small patty tins (pans). Insert the pastry rounds into the tins; press down firmly and prick the bases with a fork. Chill for at least 30 minutes.

Heat the oven to 375F/190C/Gas Mark 5. Bake the pastry for 15 minutes or until firm and pale golden in colour. Cool for a few minutes in the tins then lift on to a tray. Leave until cold.

Wash, dry and stone the cherries; use either a proper cherry stoner or insert the bent end of a new fine hairpin into the fruit and gently pull out the stones. Do this over a basin, so no juice is wasted.

Put the cherry juice, or water, with the lemon juice and redcurrant jelly into a saucepan; stir over a low heat until the jelly melts. Cool slightly.

Arrange the cherries in the cases, brush the glaze over the fruit. Leave for a short time for the glaze to stiffen, before serving.

Makes approximately 15

For the biscuit crust pastry

4 oz/100 g (1 cup) plain (all-purpose) flour

1 oz/25 g (1/4 cup) cornflour (cornstarch)

3 oz/75 g (3/8 cup) butter or margarine

2 oz/50 g (1/4 cup) caster (granulated) sugar

1 egg yolk

approximately 1/2 tablespoon water

For the filling and glaze

12 oz/350 g (3/4 lb) ripe dessert cherries

1 tablespoon (1 1/4 tbsp) cherry juice or water

1 teaspoon lemon juice

3 tablespoons (4 tbsp) redcurrant jelly

Eccles Cakes

Eccles Cakes date back to Tudor times when they were part of the fare for 'Wakes' (the Lancashire name for a holiday).
Although the festivities have changed, the cakes are still popular.

Makes 10

1 quantity Puff Pastry (see page 79)

For the filling

2 oz/50 g (1/4 cup) butter or margarine

2 oz/50 g (1/4 cup) light brown sugar

2 oz/50 g (1/3 cup) sultanas (seedless white raisins)

2 oz/50 g (1/3 cup) currants

2 tablespoons (2 1/2 tbsp) mixed candied peel, finely chopped

1 teaspoon grated lemon rind

1 tablespoon (1 1/4 tbsp) lemon juice

1/4 teaspoon mixed spice

To glaze

a little milk

approximately 1 tablespoon caster (granulated) sugar

Preheat the oven to 425-450F/220-230C/Gas Mark 7-8.

Roll out the pastry until it is very thin; cut into 10 rounds using a large saucer as a guide.

Cream the butter or margarine and sugar. Combine well with the rest of the filling ingredients. Divide the mixture between the rounds of pastry, brush the edges with a little water and gather together. Seal firmly, then turn the cakes with the joins underneath. Roll the cakes gently and shape with your fingers to make perfect rounds of about 2 1/2-3 inches/6.5-7.5 cm in diameter.

Make 2 or 3 slits on top of each cake with kitchen scissors. Brush the cakes with a very little milk and sprinkle lightly with sugar. Place on an ungreased baking (cookie) sheet and bake in the centre of the oven for 15 minutes. Reduce the heat to 350F/180C/Gas Mark 4 for a further 5-6 minutes.

To Make a Change

Banbury Cakes. Follow the recipe for Eccles Cakes, but make the pastry into oval shapes. Add 2 oz/50 g (1/2 cup) fine cake or Almond Macaroon crumbs (see page 63) to the fruits.

Macaroon Slices

These have always been a great favourite.
The crisp pastry is topped with jam (jelly), then the light macaroon mixture.
Two methods of baking are given below.

Heat the oven to 400F/200C/Gas Mark 6. Sift the flour and salt into a bowl. Rub in the butter or margarine. Add the sugar, then the egg yolk; add enough water to give a firm rolling consistency. Roll out the pastry and use to line a 10 x 7 inch (25 x 18 cm) Swiss roll tin (jelly roll pan).

If you like very crisp pastry prick it with a fork to prevent the bottom rising; bake 'blind' (without a filling) for approximately 15 minutes or until firm, but still pale in colour. Spread with the jam.

Whisk the egg whites until frothy. Add the almond essence, ground almonds and sugar. Spread this mixture carefully over the jam, sprinkle flaked almonds evenly on top. Return to the oven, lowering the heat to 350F/180C/Gas Mark 4 and cook for 15-20 minutes, or until golden brown in colour.

If you do not want to precook the pastry, you can spread the uncooked pastry with jam then add the macaroon topping. Bake for 15 minutes at the higher temperature then reduce the heat and continue cooking for a further 10-15 minutes or until the topping is firm and golden brown in colour.

Whichever method you choose, leave the cake to cool in the tin for 5 minutes then mark into slices. Remove from the tin.

Makes 16 slices

For the pastry

6 oz/175 g (1 1/2 cups) plain (all-purpose) flour

a pinch of salt

3 oz/85 g (3/8 cup) butter or margarine

1 oz/25 g (2 tbsp) caster (granulated) sugar

1 egg yolk

water to bind

For the topping

4 tablespoons (5 tbsp) sieved apricot jam (jelly)

2 egg whites

a few drops of almond essence (extract)

4 oz/110 g (1 cup) ground almonds

4 oz/110 g (1/2 cup) caster (granulated) sugar

2 oz/50 g (1/2 cup) blanched and flaked almonds

Ginger Nuts

These are typical of many similar crisp ginger biscuits (cookies) you will find throughout Britain. The best known are the Shahs of Ireland (see below) and Fairings served in the West Country.
Self-raising flour can be used in place of the plain flour and bicarbonate of soda.

Makes 10-12

4 oz/110 g (1 cup) plain (all-purpose) flour

1 level teaspoon bicarbonate of soda (baking soda)

$1/2$-1 teaspoon ground ginger

$1/2$-1 teaspoon ground cinnamon

$1/2$-1 teaspoon mixed spice

2 oz/50 g ($1/4$ cup) butter or margarine

1 oz/25 g (2 tbsp) caster (granulated) sugar

2 level tablespoons (2 $1/2$ tbsp) golden (light corn) syrup

Grease 1 or 2 baking (cookie) sheets or trays. Heat the oven to 375-400F/190-200C/Gas Mark 5-6.

Sift all the dry ingredients together very well. Put the butter or margarine, sugar and golden syrup into a saucepan. Heat gently until the butter has melted and the sugar dissolved. Add the flour mixture and blend thoroughly.

Form the mixture into 10-12 small balls; if the mixture seems slightly sticky dampen your fingers slightly. Place on the prepared sheets or trays spaced well apart. Place near the top of the oven and bake for 5 minutes. Move the sheets or trays to a lower position and reduce the heat to 325F/160C/Gas Mark 3. Bake for a further 10 minutes or until cracked on top and firm.

Allow the biscuits to become nearly cold before removing from the sheets or trays. Store in a completely airtight tin.

If you have an electric fan oven where all cooking positions have the same heat, then set the oven to 325F/160C/Gas Mark 3 and bake without changing either setting or position in the oven.

To Make a Change

Shah Biscuits. The above recipe differs from the Irish one, which includes egg, but you will have much the same result if you put pieces of candied peel and/or raisins on the biscuits before baking.

Teatime in Scotland

According to the fascinating book *The Scots Kitchen,* by F. Marian McNeill, originally published in 1929, teatime in Scotland reached as high a point of perfection in the nineteenth century as the renowned Scottish breakfast. We read that 'cakes apart, visitors were surprised at the variety of scones and light teabreads'. The book paints a picture of an elegant tea table beside a glowing fire and continues 'for many of us this made the tea hour the pleasantest hour of the day'.

Lavish farmhouse teas were also described; the contemporary English teatime meal is referred to as an inferior competitor. Whatever the truth of it, it's a sign of the enduring Scottish national pride in their splendid baking.

Traditional teas in Scotland are still as lavish and delightful as ever.

'I don't want any more hugs;
Make me some fresh tea...'

It's No Use Raising a Shout
W. H. Auden (1907-1973)

Scotch Pancakes

These thick soft pancakes, often known as 'Drop Scones' because the
mixture is dropped from a spoon on to the heated surface,
are an irresistible teatime favourite. They are best eaten on the day they are prepared.

Makes 12-15

4 oz/100 g (1 cup) self-raising
 flour or plain (all-purpose)
 flour sifted with 1 teaspoon
 baking powder

a pinch of salt

1 egg, beaten lightly

1/4 pint/150 ml (2/3 cup) milk

1 oz/25 g (2 tbsp) butter or
 margarine, melted, optional

1 tablespoon caster
 (granulated) sugar, optional

Sift the flour, or flour and baking powder, with the salt into a bowl. Make a well in the centre. Add the egg, then gradually beat in the milk. Whisk until a smooth batter is formed. The butter or margarine can be added just before cooking to make a softer and slightly richer pancake. The sugar is a matter of personal taste; add with the butter or margarine.

Lightly grease a griddle or heavy frying pan (skillet) and preheat. To test, drop a teaspoon of the mixture on to the hot surface. It should set within 1 minute. Place spoonfuls of batter on the griddle and cook for approximately 2 minutes, or until the top is covered with bubbles. Using a palette knife (spatula), turn the first pancake over and cook for 2 minutes more. Repeat with all the pancakes.

To test if the pancakes are ready, press the side gently but firmly with the blunt edge of a knife. No batter should come out.

Place a clean teacloth on a wire tray and place the pancakes on top. Cover with a second teacloth to prevent them hardening.

To Make a Change

Scots Crumpets. These are thinner than Scotch Pancakes. Cream 1/4 oz/7 g (1/4 cake) fresh (compressed) yeast with 1 teaspoon sugar; add 7 fl oz/200 ml (7/8 cup) warm milk and mix well. Top with a sprinkling of flour. Leave for 10 minutes or until the surface is covered with bubbles. Sift 4 oz/100 g (1/2 cup) plain (all-purpose) flour with a pinch of salt. Add the yeast liquid, 1 egg and 1 tablespoon (1 1/4 tbsp) melted butter. Beat well for several minutes. Cover and leave at room temperature for 45 minutes or until doubled in bulk. Beat again and cook as above.

Scones

Scones are a favourite all over Britain and appreciated in other countries too.
In Australia, for example, they have the name of 'Gems' or 'Gem Scones'.
In the old days, when milk was inclined to go sour easily,
it was used in scone-making to produce a really light texture.
Nowadays, pasteurization and refrigeration have made sour milk a thing of the past.
When fresh milk was used it was traditional to blend 1/2 level teaspoon
bicarbonate of soda (baking soda) and 1 level teaspoon cream of tartar with
8 oz/225 g (2 cups) plain (all-purpose) flour.
This you can still do, but modern self-raising flour or the equivalent in baking powder
with plain (all-purpose) flour are perfectly adequate.
The secret of a good scone is to make the mixture a really soft rolling
consistency (busy cooks can just pat out the dough to the
desired thickness instead of using the rolling pin). Handle the dough quickly and bake
the scones as soon as possible after making.
It is essential that the oven is preheated adequately before baking.

There is no need to grease baking (cookie) sheets or trays. They can just be lightly floured to keep the bottom of the scones from getting too brown. Heat the oven to 425F/220C/Gas Mark 7.

Sift the flour, or flour and baking powder, with the salt into a mixing bowl. Rub in the butter or margarine. Add sufficient milk to make a soft rolling consistency. Roll or pat out the dough until approximately 3/4 inch/2 cm thick. Cut into rounds or triangles. Put on the sheets or trays.

Bake for approximately 10 minutes towards the top of the oven. To test if they are cooked simply press the sides of the scones: your fingers should not leave an impression. Place on a wire tray to cool.

To make muffins from this unsweetened scone mixture, add a little more milk to give a slightly softer texture. Divide into 6 portions, and pat them into rounds with floured hands. Bake for 15-20 minutes.

Makes approximately 12

8 oz/225 g (2 cups) self-raising flour or plain (all-purpose) flour sifted with 2 teaspoons baking powder

a pinch of salt

1-2 oz/25-50 g (2-4 tbsp) butter or margarine

milk to mix

More Scones

The following receipes demonstrate the number of delicious variations
on the basic unsweetened scone.

Sweet Scones

Add approximately 2 oz/50 g (1/4 cup) sugar to the flour and fat mixture. If you like you can sweeten and flavour the scone dough by using honey, marmalade or black treacle (molasses) instead of sugar. Blend in these sweeteners before adding the milk, so that the dough is not too wet.

Flavoured Scones

Sift up to 1 teaspoon mixed spice, cinnamon, nutmeg or other spices into the flour. Add the finely grated rind of 1 or 2 lemons or oranges. In this case use a little fruit juice, instead of all milk, to bind the dough.

Dried fruits of various kinds and candied peel can be added. Alternatively, try using a few ripe blueberries or blackcurrants.

Savoury Scones

Sift a fairly generous amount of salt, pepper and dry mustard powder with the flour. Add up to 2 oz/50 g (1/2 cup) finely grated cheese. Often cheese scones are mixed with an egg as well as milk. Scones made with strong Lancashire cheese are particularly successful. Bake at a slightly lower setting, i.e. 400F/200C/Gas Mark 6, and for a few minutes longer.

Oatmeal Scones

These are particularly good and of course extremely healthy since all forms of oatmeal provide fibre.

Use 6 oz/175 g (1 1/2 cups) flour and 2 oz/50 g (scant 1/2 cup) rolled oats in any of the recipes given here. Add 1/2 teaspoon baking powder to self-raising flour and an extra 1/2 teaspoon to plain (all-purpose) flour.

Potato Scones

Use 4 oz/100 g (1 cup) flour and 4 oz/100 g (1/2 cup) mashed potato instead of all flour. Add 1 teaspoon baking powder to self-raising flour and 1 extra teaspoon baking powder to plain (all-purpose) flour.

chocolate fudge brownies

the happy egg co.

please take a recipe card

chocolate fudge brownies

makes 10 generous brownies

Preheat oven to 180c/ 350f/ gas 4

Brownies

300g butter or margarine

4 x large happy eggs

210g caster sugar

400g plain flour

2 x teaspoon vanilla essence

115g chopped walnuts and/or pecans

105g cocoa powder

Fudgey Icing

50g butter

35g cocoa powder

½ teaspoon vanilla essence

200g sifted icing sugar

Milk to mix

To make the Brownies

1) Melt the butter then add the cocoa powder and mix well

2) Stir in the sugar

3) Beat in the happy eggs one at a time

4) Add the vanilla essence

5) Stir in the flour and nuts then mix well

6) Pour the mixture into a greased 9inch x 13inch roasting tin/tray

7) Bake for 30 minutes until firm

Whilst cooking make the Icing

1) Melt the butter in a saucepan, add the rest of the dry ingredients and the essence.. mix well

2) Slowly add a little milk till you have a spreading consistency

3) When the brownies have cooled slightly spread over the icing

Cut the cake into squares and enjoy!

Selkirk Bannock

This is one of the richer 'speckled breads', and when fresh it can be served as a cake.
Old recipes suggest you take proven bread dough and work the fats,
sugar and fruit into it. This recipe gives instructions on making the dough first.

Cream the yeast in a bowl, add the warm water and sprinkle a little flour on top. Leave for 10 minutes, or until the surface is covered with bubbles. Sift the flour and salt into a mixing bowl. Add the yeast liquid and the sugar. Melt the butter and lard so it is soft enough to incorporate into the dough, but do not let it become oily. Work the fats into the dough with a wooden spoon or with your hands. Finally work in the sultanas. Knead the dough until smooth.

To test if the dough is sufficiently kneaded, press with a floured finger. If the impression stays then extra kneading is necessary. When the dough is sufficiently kneaded, return it to the bowl, cover and allow to rise. This will take at least 1 1/2 hours in a warm place. Towards the end of this time grease and warm a flat baking (cookie) sheet or tray.

Knead the dough again and form into a large round shape. Place it on the sheet or tray, cover lightly with oiled clingfilm (plastic wrap) and leave for about 30 minutes or until almost doubled in size.

Meanwhile heat the oven to 375F/190C/Gas Mark 5. Bake the loaf in the centre of the oven for 1-1 1/4 hours. Reduce the heat to 325F/160C/Gas Mark 3 after 45 minutes. When the loaf is ready it will sound hollow if tapped on the bottom.

Makes 1 loaf

1 oz/25 g (1 cake) fresh (compressed) yeast (for time-saving yeasts, see page 50)

1/2 pint/300 ml (1 1/4 cups) warm water

1 lb/450 g (4 cups) strong (hard wheat) or plain (all-purpose) flour

1/2 teaspoon salt

4 oz/100 g (1/2 cup) caster (granulated) sugar

4 oz/100 g (1/2 cup) butter

2 oz/50 g (1/4 cup) lard (shortening)

1 lb/450 g (2 1/2 cups) sultanas (golden raisins)

Dundee Cake

This is one of the best-loved cakes in Britain. It owes its name to the important seaport on the east coast of Scotland.
Ground almonds have always been included in the cake, enhancing the flavour and keeping it moist. The flavour is best allowed to mature for at least 1 week and up to 1 month, stored in an airtight tin.

Serves 8-10

6 oz/175 g ($^3/_4$ cup) butter

6 oz/175 g ($^3/_4$ cup) caster (granulated) sugar

a little grated lemon or orange rind, optional

3 eggs, size 1 or 2 (jumbo)

8 oz/225 g (2 cups) plain (all-purpose) flour sifted with 1 teaspoon baking powder

1 oz/25 g ($^1/_4$ cup) ground almonds

2 oz/50 g ($^1/_4$ cup) glacé (candied) cherries, quartered

2 oz/50 g ($^1/_3$ cup) mixed candied peel, chopped

1 lb/450 g (3 cups) mixed dried fruit

2 tablespoons ($2^1/_2$ tbsp) sherry or milk

To decorate

1-2 oz/25-50 g ($^1/_6$-$^1/_3$ cup) blanched almonds

Grease and flour or line a 7 or 8 inch/18 or 20 cm cake tin (pan). Heat the oven to 325F/160C/Gas Mark 3.

Cream the butter and sugar until soft and light. Add the grated rind, if using. Gradually beat in the eggs; save the shells with a little egg white adhering to them. Fold the flour and baking powder into the creamed mixture then mix in all the remaining ingredients.

Spoon the mixture into the prepared tin; arrange the blanched almonds, which must be perfectly dry, in a neat design on top of the cake. Brush them with the egg white left in the shells to glaze.

Bake in the centre of the oven for 30 minutes. Reduce the temperature to 300F/150C/Gas Mark 2. If cooking the smaller cake allow a further $1^1/_2$ hours. The shallow wider cake needs another $1^3/_4$ hours. Test to see if the cake is cooked by pressing gently but firmly on top. It will have shrunk away slightly from the sides of the tin. Allow to cool in the tin for 5 minutes then turn out carefully on to a wire tray to cool completely.

Shortbread

This is one of the simplest biscuits (cookies) to prepare but one of the most delicious. Shortbread is an essential part of a good Scottish tea.

Heat the oven well ahead at low to very moderate, 300-325F/150-160C/Gas Mark 2-3. This is important to keep the shortbread a good shape. Do this while the mixture is standing in the mould (see below).

To make a real shortbread shape, dust a wooden shortbread mould with rice flour or cornflour (cornstarch).

Sift the flours into a mixing bowl. Cut the butter into pieces then rub it into the flours. Add the sugar. Turn the mixture out of the bowl and knead until smooth. Press the mixture into the mould and leave for 1 hour for the shape to set. Turn out carefully on to an ungreased baking (cookie) sheet or tray.

If you have no wooden mould, form the dough into a neat round about 1/2 inch/1.5 cm thick and flute the edges.

Prick the biscuit evenly all over with a fine skewer. Bake in the centre of the oven for 35-40 minutes until firm, but still pale. Mark into 8 triangles and leave to cool on the tray. When cold, sprinkle a little sugar on top.

To Make a Change

Petticoat Tails. One theory about this name is that these biscuits, a favourite of Mary Queen of Scots, were called after fashionable skirts of the day. Make the shortbread mixture but roll it out until only 1/4 inch/6 mm thick. Form into two rounds. Place on greased sheets or trays, mark in triangles and dust with caster sugar. Bake for only 15 minutes. Separate the triangles before the biscuits are cold. Dust with sugar.

Makes 8

4 oz/100 g (1 cup) plain (all-purpose) flour

2 oz/50 g (scant 1/2 cup) rice flour or ground rice or cornflour (cornstarch)

4 oz/100 g (1/2 cup) butter

2 oz/50 g (1/2 cup) caster (granulated) sugar

To decorate

a little caster (granulated) sugar

Teatime in Wales

A line from a well-loved song from Wales (Cymru) announces:

We'll keep a welcome on the hillside
We'll keep a welcome in the dales

and there is no doubt that the hospitable inhabitants of this principality have always enjoyed entertaining.

The mountains that separate Wales from England made travel rather difficult in the past, so supplies of exotic foods would not have been readily available in remote areas. That is why much of the traditional teatime cooking of Wales depends upon dried fruit, caraway seeds and food that can be stored, and why strong Welsh traditions have developed and been retained. Most cooking in Wales depends upon home-grown ingredients.

Bara is the Welsh name for bread, of which there are various types. The best known, of course, is the speckled bread – Bara Brith – for which the recipe is opposite.

Here though, great Anna! whom three realms obey,
Dost sometimes counsel take – and sometimes Tea.

The Rape of The Lock, Alexander Pope (1688-1744) (on Queen Anne)

Bara Brith

This is the famous Welsh 'speckled bread',
related to the Selkirk Bannock of Scotland and Ireland's richer Barm Breac,
or Barm Brack (see pages 89 and 100).

Cream the yeast in a bowl and blend in the milk, or milk and water. Sprinkle over a little flour and leave for 10 minutes, or until the surface is covered with bubbles. Meanwhile sift the flour, salt and spice into a large bowl. Rub in the lard or butter and add the sugar. Stir in the yeast liquid. Mix well. Add the egg and dried fruits and blend well.

Turn the dough out on to a floured surface and knead until smooth. Return to the bowl, cover and leave for about 1 1/2 hours, or until the dough has almost doubled in size. Turn out of the bowl and knead again. During this proving process grease and warm a 2 1/2 lb/1.2 kg loaf tin (pan) or a baking (cookie) sheet or tray.

Mould the dough to fit the tin or make a neat oblong and place it on the sheet or tray. Cover lightly with oiled cling film (plastic wrap). Leave for 30 minutes, or until almost doubled in size.

Meanwhile heat the oven to 375F/190C/Gas Mark 5. Bake the loaf in the centre of the oven for 45 minutes; if necessary reduce the heat slightly for the last 10-15 minutes. The loaf is ready if it sounds hollow when tapped on the bottom. Brush the loaf with honey to give a pleasing shine.

Makes 1 loaf

3/4 oz/20 g (3/4 cake) fresh (compressed) yeast (for time-saving yeasts, see page 50)

8 fl oz/225 ml (1 cup) warm milk, or milk and water

12 oz/350 g (3 cups) strong (hard wheat) or plain (all-purpose) flour

1/2 teaspoon salt

1/2-1 teaspoon ground mixed spice

2 oz/50 g (1/4 cup) lard (shortening) or butter

2 oz/50 g (1/4 cup) sugar, preferably brown

1 egg

8 oz/225 g (1 1/4 cups) currants

6 oz/175 g (1 cup) seedless raisins or sultanas (golden raisins)

2-3 tablespoons (2 1/2-3 3/4 tbsp) chopped mixed candied peel

To glaze

a little honey, warmed, optional

Bara Carane

Seed cakes have been popular for generations, particularly in Wales.
The flavour of this Welsh seed loaf is enhanced by the addition
of candied orange peel and orange flower water (available from chemists).

Serves 8

8 oz/225 g (1 cup) butter or
margarine

8 oz/225 g (1 cup) caster
(granulated) sugar

1 teaspoon orange flower water

3 eggs

10 oz/300 g (2 1/2 cups) self-
raising flour or plain (all-
purpose) flour sifted with 2 1/2
teaspoons baking powder

1 teaspoon caraway seeds

3 oz/75 g (scant 1/2 cup)
candied orange peel, finely
chopped

4 tablespoons (5 tbsp) milk

For the topping

1 tablespoon (1 1/4 tbsp) caster
(granulated) sugar

1/2 teaspoon caraway seeds

Grease and flour or line a 2 1/2 lb/1.2 kg loaf tin (pan). Heat the oven to 325F/160C/Gas Mark 3.

Cream the butter or margarine and sugar with the orange flower water until soft and light. Gradually beat in the eggs then fold in the flour, or flour and baking powder, the caraway seeds and candied peel. Stir in the milk gradually to give a soft consistency.

Spoon the mixture into the prepared tin and sprinkle the caster sugar and caraway seeds on top. Bake the cake in the centre of the oven for 1 hour. Reduce the temperature to 300F/150C/Gas Mark 2 and cook for a further 20-30 minutes, or until firm to a gentle touch. Turn out and cool.

Pour, varlet, pour the water, The water steaming hot!
A spoonful for each man of us, Another for the pot!

Barry Pain (1864-1928)

Welsh Cakes – *Pice ar y Maen*

I often think that the appearance of these flat cakes belies their delicious flavour.
No true Welsh tea is complete without them.
Currants are always included, but I like to add some seedless raisins too.

Sift the flour, or flour and baking powder, and salt into a bowl. Rub in the butter or margarine. Add the sugar and currants. Mix in the egg and enough milk to make a soft rolling consistency. Roll out on a lightly floured board until the dough is about 1/2 inch/1.5 cm in thickness. Cut into small rounds with a pastry cutter.

Preheat and lightly grease the griddle, which in Wales is sometimes called a 'bakestone'. When it is ready, a little flour shaken on top will take at least 1 minute to turn golden brown. Alternatively, use a greased heavy frying pan (skillet).

Put the cakes on to the hot surface and cook for 8-10 minutes, turning once, until they are golden brown on both sides. Transfer to a wire tray to cool. When cold, dust with a little sugar.

Makes 16-18

8 oz/225 g (2 cups) self-raising flour or plain (all-purpose) flour sifted with 2 teaspoons baking powder

a pinch of salt

4 oz/110 g (1/2 cup) butter or margarine

4 oz/110 g (1/2 cup) caster (granulated) sugar

4 oz/100 g (2/3 cup) currants, or a mixture of currants and seedless raisins

l egg

a little milk to bind

To decorate

caster (granulated) sugar

Teisen Berffro

These crisp cakes are a speciality of Aberffraw, on Caernarvon Bay
in beautiful Anglesey. The dough is moulded around scallop shells before baking.
Scallops, like other shellfish, are plentiful off the Welsh coast.

Makes 12

4 oz/100 g (1/2 cup) caster
  (granulated) sugar

4 oz/100 g (1/2 cup) butter,
  preferably unsalted (sweet)

6 oz/175 g (3/4 cup) plain (all-
  purpose) flour

Lightly grease 2 flat baking (cookie) sheets or trays. Heat the oven to 350-375F/180-190C/Gas Mark 4-5.

Put 1 oz/25 g (2 tbsp) of the sugar on one side. Add the rest to the butter and cream until soft and light. Add the flour and knead well with your hands until blended. Divide into 12 portions.

Sprinkle a little of the reserved sugar into a scallop shell or over the back of the shell if you prefer to mould the dough on that side. Flatten one portion of the dough and press it against the sugared surface until it has acquired the shape. Gently remove the pastry shell and place it on the sheet or tray. Repeat with the remaining portions. If the shells are large you can mould over the centre part only, but try to make a neat edge.

Bake for 15 minutes at the higher setting; if your oven is inclined to be rather hot, it is better to use the lower setting and bake for 20 minutes. They should be crisp and golden. Cool then remove from the sheets or trays.

Serve cold, plain, or dusted with sifted icing (confectioners') sugar or filled with jam (jelly) and whipped cream just before serving.

To Make a Change

Rich Berffro Cakes. You will need 10-12 small scallop shells. Increase the quantity of sugar and butter to equal the flour, i.e. 6 oz/175 g (3/4 cup) of each. Follow the method above but grease the inside of the scallop shells and press the mixture into them. Preheat the oven to very moderate, 325F/160C/Gas Mark 3 and bake the cakes for 15-20 minutes. Cool slightly then remove carefully from the shells. Dust with caster sugar.

Teatime in Ireland

The selection of cakes and pastries offered by Ireland is as wide as that in any other part of Britain but traditional Irish breads are so delicious, and so very easy to make, that I have concentrated mainly on these.

The Irish affection for and dependence on potatoes as an important ingredient in their cooking is reflected in the way they use them not only as part of the day's main meal but also in teatime foods. The Boxty Bread, which is equally good made with a sweet or savoury bias, is a case in point. You may be surprised to find potatoes in a cake recipe, but that is not unusual in Ireland: they give a light texture and pleasant flavour to the cake. The Irish are not alone in using potatoes as an ingredient in baking: many other European countries use potato flour in baking to lighten the dough.

 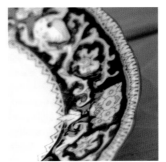 

Love and scandal are the best sweeteners of tea.

Love in Several Masques, Henry Fielding (1707-1754)

Irish Soda Bread

No Irish teatime would be complete without slices of this light, delicious bread
spread with incomparable Irish butter.
It can be cooked in the oven or on a griddle. Buttermilk is the liquid left after
making butter, low in fat and slightly salty. If you cannot obtain it
use skimmed milk and double the quantity of cream of tartar.

Makes 1 or 2 loaves

1 lb/450 g (4 cups) plain (all-purpose) flour

1/2-1 teaspoon salt

1/2 teaspoon bicarbonate of soda (baking soda)

1/2 teaspoon cream of tartar

approximately 1/2 pint/300 ml (1 1/4 cups) buttermilk

Lightly grease 1 or 2 flat baking (cookie) sheets or trays. Heat the oven to 425F/220C/Gas Mark 7.

Sift all the dry ingredients into a mixing bowl. Gradually blend in the buttermilk. Different flours vary a little in the amount of liquid they absorb. The dough should be soft in texture but easy to handle. Knead lightly until smooth.

Form the dough into 1 or 2 rounds about 1-1 1/2 inches/2.5-3.5 cm thick. Place on the baking sheets or trays. Mark each round into quarters, known as 'farls'. You could mark the large round into eight, if liked. Bake 1 large loaf for 30 minutes, 2 small ones for 20-25 minutes. After about 15-20 minutes reduce the temperature slightly if the bread is getting too brown.

To cook the bread on a griddle, preheat, but do not grease, the griddle. It is the right heat when dry flour turns golden in colour within 1 1/2-2 minutes. Form the dough into 1 or 2 thinner rounds, about 3/4 inch/2 cm thick. Mark in farls very gently. Place on the griddle and cook for 6-7 minutes on each side, turning once.

The Modern Touch

If you prefer not to eat white bread, use wholemeal (wholewheat) or brown flour, both of which make delicious Soda Breads. You will need a little extra milk to give the correct balance as both these flours absorb more liquid. As a result the cooking time will be a few minutes longer than given in the recipe.

Boxty Bread

One might say that the word 'Boxty' is synonymous with the Irish love of potatoes. The basic mixture below for a baked bread can also be cooked on a griddle in the same way as Soda Bread (page 98) or made into pancakes or dumplings. Use bacon fat instead of butter for a more savoury flavour.

Lightly grease a flat baking (cookie) sheet or tray. Heat the oven to 325-350F/160-180C/Gas Mark 3-4. Choose the lower setting if your oven is on the hot side, for Boxty must be baked steadily.

Grate (grind) the raw potatoes by hand or in a food processor. Place in a cloth and squeeze very firmly over a basin to catch the liquid. Leave to stand. Mix the grated potatoes with the mashed potatoes immediately so they do not discolour. Add the butter or bacon fat.

Gradually work in the flour and seasoning to taste. Carefully pour away the potato liquid from the basin, leaving the starch sediment behind. Add the starch to the flour and potato mixture, and combine well. Place the mixture on a floured board and form into a round 1/2 inch/1.5 cm in thickness. Place on the prepared sheet or tray and mark into 8 sections (farls). Bake for 40-45 minutes, or until firm.

Serve freshly cooked or, better still, really hot, with butter.

To Make a Change

Boxty Pancakes. Omit the butter or bacon fat. Sift 1/2 teaspoon bicarbonate of soda (baking soda) into the flour. Blend with enough buttermilk or ordinary milk to make a thick batter. Heat a little fat in a strong frying pan (skillet). Drop tablespoons of the batter into the hot fat. Cook steadily for 4 minutes or until firm underneath, then turn and cook the other side for the same time.

Serve hot spread with butter, or butter and sugar.

Makes 1 loaf

8 oz/225 g (1/2 lb) uncooked potatoes, weight when peeled

8 oz/225 g (1 cup) cooked and mashed potatoes

2 oz/50 g (1/4 cup) butter or bacon fat, melted

2 oz/50 g (1/2 cup) plain (all-purpose) flour

salt to taste

pepper to taste

Barm Brack

Barm Brack or Breac is a celebration Irish bread, made for Hallowe'en.
Often a ring, wrapped in paper, is baked in the bread.
Tradition has it that whoever finds the ring will be married within a year.
Use plain (all-purpose) flour rather than strong (hard wheat) flour
as the texture should be more like a cake.

Makes 1 loaf

3/4 oz/20 g (3/4 cake) fresh (compressed) yeast (for time-saving yeasts, see page 50)

8 fl oz/225 ml (1 cup) warm milk

12 oz/350 g (3 cups) plain (all-purpose) flour

1 teaspoon ground or grated nutmeg

4 oz/100 g (1/2 cup) butter or margarine

1-2 teaspoons caraway seeds, optional

4 oz/110 g (1/2 cup) caster (granulated) sugar

8 oz/225 g (1 1/4 cups) currants

8 oz/225 g (1 1/4 cups) seedless raisins

4 oz/100 g (3/4 cup) mixed candied peel, finely chopped

2 eggs, size 1 or 2 (jumbo) or 3 smaller eggs

Cream the yeast in a bowl and blend in the milk. Sprinkle over a little of the flour. Leave for 10 minutes, or until the surface is covered with bubbles. Meanwhile sift the flour and nutmeg into a large bowl. Rub in the butter or margarine and add the caraway seeds and sugar. Stir in the yeast liquid, mixing well. Add the fruit, peel and finally the eggs. Blend the mixture thoroughly. Turn out on to a lightly floured surface and knead the dough. If it seems a little soft, flour your hands; gradually the dough will become more manageable. Knead until smooth then return to the bowl, cover and leave for about 1 1/2 hours, or until doubled in size. Turn out and knead again until smooth and no impression is left when pressed with a floured finger. While the dough is proving (rising), grease and warm a 9 inch/23 cm round cake tin (pan). Mould the dough to fit into the tin. Cover and leave until nearly doubled in size.

Meanwhile heat the oven to 375F/190C/Gas Mark 5. Bake the loaf for 1-1 1/4 hours. Reduce the temperature to 325F/160C/Gas Mark 3 after 45 minutes. When the loaf is cooked it will sound hollow when tapped on the bottom.

When fresh this fruit bread can be served as a cake.

Treacle Bread

The majority of Irish breads are not made with yeast,
so they are quick and easy to prepare. Treacle Bread is best served hot or warm
with plenty of butter. If you cannot obtain buttermilk,
omit the bicarbonate of soda and use ordinary milk with self-raising flour.

Lightly grease 1 or 2 baking (cookie) sheets or trays. As treacle burns if the oven is too hot, preheat to moderately hot, 400F/200C/Gas Mark 6.

Sift all the dry ingredients into a bowl. Rub in the butter or margarine. Add the sugar and treacle and mix very well. Gradually add enough buttermilk to make a dough that is soft in texture, but easy to handle. Knead lightly until smooth.

Form the dough into two rounds each about 1-1 1/2 inches/2.5-3.5 cm thick. Place on the baking sheet(s) or tray(s). Mark into quarters (farls). Bake for 20-25 minutes and reduce the heat slightly after 15 minutes.

To cook the loaves on a griddle, grease the griddle lightly before preheating. For testing the griddle and cooking the bread see Irish Soda Bread, page 98.

Makes 2 loaves

1 lb/450 g (4 cups) plain (all-purpose) flour

1/2-1 teaspoon salt

1/2 teaspoon bicarbonate of soda (baking soda)

a pinch of ground ginger, optional

2 oz/50 g (1/4 cup) butter or margarine

2 oz/50 g (1/4 cup) caster (granulated) sugar

2 tablespoons (2 1/2 tbsp) black treacle (molasses)

buttermilk to mix

Nursery Teas

Even though few modern homes boast a day nursery and most children have tea with the rest of the family, the idea of a 'nursery tea' is still inviting. Perhaps it's time for the custom to be revived – and not only for the children!

Once upon a time children were instructed to eat up all their bread and butter before they were allowed to eat cake. Children do not have to be so restrained these days, but many of them really enjoy bread and butter. Savoury sandwiches are a great favourite, especially if they are thin, cut into triangles or other shapes and have the crusts removed.

Children love individual one-portion foods, such as Cup Cakes (page 104) and Scotch Pancakes (page 86). Miniature versions of both can be made for a dolls' tea party or teddy bears' picnic.

'Take some more tea', the March Hare said to Alice, very earnestly.

Alice in Wonderland, Lewis Carroll (1832-1898)

Sponge Cake

This is the true sponge, often called a fatless sponge.
It is ideal for young children and it can be iced for a birthday or other special
occasion (see page 105). Plain flour is used as the mixture is aerated by
whisking the eggs and sugar, but if you have not made this type of sponge before,
you could use self-raising flour to ensure the mixture rises.

Grease and flour or line an 8 inch/20 cm cake tin (pan). As this cake is inclined to stick prepare the tin very carefully. Heat the oven to 350F/180C/Gas Mark 4.

Sift the flour on to a flat plate and leave in a warm place while whisking the eggs and sugar; this lightens the flour.

Put the eggs and sugar into a mixing bowl, or the bowl of an electric mixer, and whisk until the mixture is thick and creamy; you should be able to see the trail of the whisk.

Sift the flour into the egg mixture and fold it in carefully and thoroughly and bake for 35-40 minutes or until the sponge is firm to gentle pressure. Finally fold in the hot water. Spoon the mixture into the prepared tin.

Cool for 2-3 minutes in the tin then carefully invert on to a wire tray to cool, away from draughts. Sprinkle with sugar.

Serves 6-8

4 oz/110 g (1 cup) flour, plain (all-purpose) or self-raising

4 eggs, size 1 or 2 (jumbo)

5 oz/150 g (generous 1/2 cup) caster (granulated) sugar

1/2 tablespoon hot water

To decorate

a little caster (granulated) or icing (confectioners') sugar

Cup Cakes

These are ideal for a nursery tea.
The quantity given refers to the cakes made in average-sized paper cases.
If entertaining very small children bake the cakes in
the tiny cases used for petits-fours and reduce the cooking time.
For a special occasion the cakes could be decorated with miniature
edible cake decorations.

Makes 20-24

4 oz/110 g ($1/2$ cup) butter or
margarine

4 oz/110 g ($1/2$ cup) caster
(granulated) sugar

2 eggs, size 1 or 2 (jumbo)

4 oz/110 g (1 cup) self-raising
flour or plain (all-purpose)
flour sifted with 1 teaspoon
baking powder

For the topping

Glacé Icing, made with
8 oz/225 g (2 cups) icing
(confectioners') sugar (see
page 105)

Put 20-24 paper cases into patty tins; these are not essential, but support the paper cases as the cakes rise in cooking. Heat the oven to 400F/200C/ Gas Mark 6.

Cream the butter or margarine and sugar until soft and light. Gradually beat in the eggs. Fold in the flour, and baking powder if used. Spoon the mixture into the paper cases, filling them only half full, for the cakes rise in baking.

Bake towards the top of the oven for 10 minutes or until firm to the touch. Allow to become quite cold. Make the icing and spoon it over the cakes. Leave until set.

The Modern Touch

Busy mothers will be grateful for the modern soft margarines that cream so easily. If you prefer to use butter, do not melt it but leave at room temperature until soft enough to cream.

All-in-One Cup Cakes. Put all the ingredients into a bowl. Beat by hand for about 2 minutes or allow 1 minute in an electric mixer or 30 seconds in a food processor. There is no need to use extra baking powder in this recipe for you do not want the cakes to rise too dramatically.

Chocolate Icing

The small amount of butter in this icing gives a softer texture
but as it is not too rich it is ideal for children. This would cover the top of the
Sponge Cake (see page 103) or a thin topping on 12 small cakes.

Blend the butter, sugar and cocoa together until smooth. Gradually blend in enough warm water to make a soft consistency.

1 oz/25 g (2 tbsp) butter, melted and cooled

8 oz/225 g (2 cups) icing (confectioners') sugar, sifted

1 oz/25 g (1/4 cup) cocoa powder (unsweetened cocoa), sifted

a little warm water

Glacé Icing

This is sometimes known as 'water icing', because the icing (confectioners')
sugar is blended with water.
It can be coloured with food colouring or flavoured as desired.

If you have time for the icing to stand, about 15 minutes, there is no need to sift the sugar for the lumps come out in time. If using at once then the sugar must be sifted.

Blend the sugar and water together. You have a better texture if you use warm or even hot water, but this does mean waiting for the icing to cool before spreading on the cake.

8 oz/225 g (2 cups) icing (confectioners') sugar

approximately 1 1/4 tablespoons (good 1 1/2 tbsp) warm water

Gingerbread Men

For generations children have loved these crisp biscuits (cookies).
If the children are very young it would be wise to use less ginger than suggested
in the recipe. The cakes keep well in an airtight tin.

Makes 10

3 oz/75 g ($^3/_8$ cup) butter or margarine

3 oz/75 g ($^3/_8$ cup) caster (granulated) or light brown sugar

3 oz/75 g ($^1/_4$ cup) golden (light corn) syrup

1-2 teaspoons ground ginger

8 oz/225 g (2 cups) plain (all-purpose) flour

l egg

a little milk to bind

To decorate

20 currants

glacé (candied) cherries or sweets

a little Glacé Icing (see page 105), optional

Grease 2 flat baking (cookie) sheets or trays. As these crisp biscuit type cakes take a little while to prepare, preheat the oven when they are almost ready for baking, setting it to 350F/180C/Gas Mark 4.

Put the butter or margarine, sugar and syrup into a saucepan and place over a low heat to melt. Sift the ginger with the flour, add to the melted ingredients and mix thoroughly. Add the egg and blend well. Very gradually add enough milk to bind the mixture. This should be sufficiently firm to roll out without difficulty, for it is advisable to use the minimum amount of flour on the pastry board or working surface.

If you do not have a cutter in the shape of a man, draw and cut out a shape in thick paper or cardboard and use as a pattern to cut round.

Roll out the dough until it is approximately $^1/_4$ inch/6 mm in thickness and cut out the shapes. Place them carefully on the sheets or trays. Press currants in place for eyes and small pieces of glacé cherry for the nose and mouth. To make buttons down the bodies use glacé cherries or make them with sweets stuck in place with glacé icing when the shapes are cooked and cool. You could also use sweets for the mouths.

Bake for 12-15 minutes or until firm to the touch; do not make them too crisp, for they harden as they cool. When cold, decorate further if desired.

Flapjacks

Flapjacks are very popular with both children and adults, and easy to make. The oats provide an excellent source of fibre to offset the sweetness of the sugar and syrup.

Grease a 7-8 inch/18-20 cm square tin (pan) very well. Heat the oven to 350F/180C/Gas Mark 4.

Put the butter or margarine, sugar and syrup into a saucepan. Stir over a low heat until the fat has melted. Remove the pan from the heat. Add the rolled oats and blend thoroughly with the melted ingredients.

Spoon the mixture into the prepared tin and smooth the surface quite flat. Bake for approximately 25 minutes or until evenly golden brown. Allow to cool for a few minutes then mark in fingers or squares. When the biscuits are almost cold remove from the tin.

Store flapjacks in an airtight tin by themselves. If stored with other biscuits (cookies) they tend to soften.

To Make a Change
Top some of the flapjacks with melted milk or plain (semi-sweet) chocolate. Allow to set.

Makes 12-16

3 oz/85 g ($^3/_8$ cup) butter or margarine

3 oz/85 g ($^3/_8$ cup) caster (granulated) sugar

1 tablespoon (1$^1/_4$ tbsp) golden (light corn) syrup

6 oz/175 g (scant 2 cups) rolled oats

'Woman is like a teabag
– you can't tell how strong she is until you put her in hot water.'

1981, Nancy Reagan, wife of the then President of the USA

Teatime
Around the World

The pleasure of teatime - the best imaginable way of bridging the gap
between lunch and the evening meal - has been adopted in many parts of the world,
especially where part of the population is of British descent.
On the table will be a pleasant combination of dishes made from well-loved recipes
handed down through the generations from the 'old country' and new
and exciting ideas which clever cooks have created from the produce
particular to their region.

In Australia and South Africa, tropical fruits are frequently used to add
flavour to cakes. If you have never tasted a light cake
in which crushed pineapple is an ingredient, you have a real treat in store
with the sponge recipe on page 112.
I have attributed Passion Fruit Pavlova on page 113 to Australia.
This meringue cake is just as popular in New Zealand, however, where kiwi fruit
may well be used instead of passion fruit.

The farming communities of New Zealand tuck in to really substantial teas.
Fruit cakes are a great favourite:
see some typical recipes on pages 122 and 123.
One of these cakes is full of crystallized fruit, which turns it into a real luxury.

South African teatime goodies are a happy marriage of British
and Dutch recipes, the latter typified by the deep-fried cakes on page 126,
and many make good use of the succulent fruits of the Cape.

Canadian dishes are often as sumptuous as those of the United States,
with some interesting extras brought into the country by
various European communities, such as the Chocolate Cake on page 115.
From the USA I have included two classic American cakes
– Devil's Food Cake and Lady Baltimore Cake. You will find these, with other
equally good but less familiar recipes, on pages 129 to 130.

Apricot Ginger Gâteau

This has the texture of a true gingerbread and the fresh taste of apricots.

Line a 7 1/2 inch/19 cm square cake tin (pan) with greased greaseproof (wax) paper. Heat the oven to 325F/160C/Gas Mark 3.

Sift the dry ingredients into a mixing bowl. Put the butter or margarine, sugar and golden syrup into a saucepan over a moderate heat until melted. Blend with the flour mixture. Add the eggs and chopped ginger to the mixture. Blend thoroughly. Spoon into the prepared tin and bake for 1 hour or until firm to the touch. Allow to cool in the tin.

Place the ginger syrup, water and sugar into a saucepan and heat slowly until the sugar has dissolved. Poach the apricots gently in the syrup, turning them once or twice. Lift out 8 halves for the topping; continue cooking the remainder until they form a stiff purée. Leave to cool. Whip the cream. Split the cake and sandwich together with a little cream and half the purée. Top with the remaining purée then top with some of the cream. Decorate with halved apricots and a piping of the remaining cream.

Serves 8

For the cake

8 oz/225 g (2 cups) plain (all-purpose) flour

1 teaspoon baking powder

1/2 teaspoon bicarbonate of soda (baking soda)

1/2-1 teaspoon ground ginger

4 oz/110 g (1/2 cup) butter or margarine

4 oz/110 g (scant 1/2 cup) light brown sugar

6 oz/175 g (1/2 cup) golden (light corn) syrup

2 eggs, beaten

2 oz/50 g (1/4 cup) preserved ginger, well drained and finely chopped

For the filling and topping

2 tablespoons (2 1/2 tbsp) syrup from preserved ginger

1 tablespoon (1 1/4 tbsp) water

2 oz/50 g (1/4 cup) caster (granulated) sugar, or to taste

1 1/4 lb/550 g (1 1/4 lb) ripe apricots, halved and stoned

1/2 pint/300 ml (1 1/4 cups) double (heavy) cream

Crushed Pineapple Sponge

This is a delicious, light sponge-type cake; although the amount of fat used is small, the sponge keeps well if made with canned pineapple.
If you prefer to use fresh pineapple, then eat the sponge on the day it is baked.

Serves 6-8

1 x 1 lb/453 g (1 lb) can pineapple rings or crushed pineapple in syrup or natural juice (see method)

10 oz/300 g (2 1/2 cups) self-raising flour or plain (all-purpose) flour sifted with 2 1/2 teaspoons baking powder

2 oz/50 g (1/4 cup) butter or margarine

6-8 oz/175-225 g (3/4 to 1 cup) caster (granulated) sugar

2 eggs

2 tablespoons (2 1/2 tbsp) pineapple liquid, plus another

2 tablespoons (2 1/2 tbsp) pineapple liquid or milk or lemon juice

For the filling and decoration

pineapple or apricot jam (jelly)

whipped cream

pineapple segments

chopped nuts or shredded fresh coconut or desiccated coconut

Line the base of two 8 inch/20 cm sponge sandwich tins (layer pans); grease and flour the sides well. Heat the oven to 350F/180C/Gas Mark 4.

Strain the canned pineapple and chop enough to fill a 1/2 pint/300 ml (1 1/4 cup) measure. If using crushed pineapple, strain and measure out the same amount of fruit. Keep the liquid from the can.

Sift the flour, or flour and baking powder, into a bowl. Rub in the butter or margarine. Add the rest of the ingredients. Use the higher amount of sugar with pineapple canned in natural juice (unsweetened). The lemon juice gives a distinctly sharp taste to the sponge.

Divide the mixture evenly between the sandwich tins. Bake for 30 minutes, or until firm to the touch. The cakes remain pale in colour even when cooked. Turn out carefully and allow to become quite cold. Remove the lining paper.

Sandwich the cakes with a little jam, whipped cream and pineapple segments. Top with more whipped cream, if liked, pineapple segments and chopped nuts or coconut.

Passion Fruit Pavlova

This meringue shape, which is now internationally popular,
is equally good as a gâteau for tea as it is for a special dessert. The fruit can be
varied according to the time of year.

Cut a round of greaseproof (wax) paper, baking parchment or non-stick silicone paper 9-10 inches/23-25 cm in diameter. Put this on a flat baking (cookie) tray. Preheat the oven. If you want the Pavlova to be very crisp, like an ordinary meringue, set it very low, 200F/110C/Gas Mark 0 or 1/4 or S. To follow the Australian method, preheat to moderate, or even moderately hot, if your oven is gentle, i.e. 350-375F/180-190C/ Gas Mark 4-5. This produces a meringue with a slightly marshmallow texture inside.

Whisk the egg whites until very stiff, but do not allow them to become dry and crumbly. Fold in the vanilla essence and vinegar. Blend the sugar and cornflour. Gradually beat half the sugar into the egg whites, then fold in the remainder.

Spread part of the meringue mixture over the paper, then spoon or pipe the remainder around the sides to give a flan shape. If using the higher heat bake for 7 or 8 minutes then immediately reduce the heat to the lower temperature; bake for about 2-2 1/2 hours. If using a constant lower setting allow about 2 1/2-3 hours. Leave to cool, and remove the paper very carefully.

For the filling, whip the cream until it just stands in peaks. Set a little aside for piping. Blend the pulp of 4 passion fruit with the cream and add sugar if liked. To keep the Pavlova crisp, add the filling just before serving. Pipe the remaining cream on top and spoon over the remaining passion fruit pulp.

Serves 8

6 egg whites

1/4 teaspoon vanilla essence (extract)

1 1/2 teaspoons white vinegar

12 oz/350 g (1/2 cups) caster (granulated) sugar

1 teaspoon cornflour (cornstarch)

For the filling

1/2 pint/300 ml (1 1/4 cups) double (heavy) cream

6 passion fruit

a little sugar, if desired

Lamingtons

These are squares of light plain sponge coated with a chocolate icing and coconut.
They are a favourite with both children and adults
and deserve to be better known outside Australia. The jam (jelly)
filling is not essential, but it makes the cake more moist.
Make triangles or round shapes if you prefer.

Makes 12-16

For the cake

5 oz/150 g (5/8 cup) butter or margarine

6 oz/175 g (3/4 cup) caster (granulated) sugar

1/4 teaspoon vanilla essence (extract)

2 eggs

8 oz/225 g (2 cups) self-raising flour or plain (all-purpose) flour sifted with 1 1/2 teaspoons baking powder

a little milk to mix

4 tablespoons (5 tbsp) apricot jam (jelly), optional

For the coating

approximately 4 oz/100 g (1 1/4 cups) desiccated (shredded) coconut

Chocolate Icing, made with 8 oz/225 g (2 cups) icing (confectioners') sugar (see page 105)

Grease and flour or line a 9 inch/23 cm square cake tin (pan). Heat the oven to 350F/180C/Gas Mark 4.

Cream the butter or margarine, sugar and vanilla essence until soft and light. Gradually beat in the eggs, then fold in the flour, or flour and baking powder, with enough milk to make a soft consistency. Spoon into the prepared tin and smooth flat on top.

Bake for 35-40 minutes, or until firm to the touch. Transfer to a wire tray to cool. When cold, remove the paper. If using jam, split the cake horizontally, spread one layer with jam and put the 2 together again. Cut into 12 or 16 squares.

Scatter the coconut on to a flat surface. Make up the icing. Using a fine fork, carefully lift one portion of cake and dip in the icing to give a thin coating on all sides. Turn in the coconut. Repeat with the remaining cakes. Place on a wire tray with a large dish underneath to catch any drips of icing and leave to set.

Chocolate Cake

The population of Canada is very cosmopolitan,
which is why its food is so varied and interesting. This cake, the recipe for which
was given to me by a Canadian friend,
certainly has the moist texture one associates with classic European cakes.

Grease and flour or line two really deep 8-9 inch/20-23 cm sandwich tins (layer pans).

Pour the boiling water over the chocolate and cocoa powder and stir until the chocolate melts. Leave to cool. During this period heat the oven to 350F/180C/Gas Mark 4.

Cream the butter or margarine, sugar and vanilla essence until soft and light. Separate the eggs and beat the yolks into the creamed mixture. Sift the flour with the baking powder and bicarbonate of soda. Fold into the creamed mixture alternately with the chocolate mixture and yoghurt.

Whisk the egg whites until just stiff, do not allow these to become dry and crumbly. Fold the egg whites into the mixture and spoon into the prepared tins.

Bake for 35-40 minutes, or until firm to the touch. Allow to cool for 2-3 minutes then remove from the tins and place on a wire tray to cool. When cold, fill and top with the Chocolate Nut Frosting.

Serves 8

8 fl oz/225 ml (1 cup) boiling water

5 oz/150 g (5 squares) plain (semi-sweet) chocolate, broken into small pieces

1 oz/25 g ($1/4$ cup) cocoa powder (unsweetened cocoa), sifted

8 oz/225 g (1 cup) butter or margarine

9 oz/250 g (1 $1/8$ cup) caster (granulated) sugar

$1/2$ teaspoon vanilla essence (extract)

3 eggs, size 1 or 2 (jumbo)

10 oz/300 g (2 $1/2$ cups) plain (all-purpose) flour

1 teaspoon baking powder

$1/2$ teaspoon bicarbonate of soda (baking soda)

$1/4$ pint/150 ml ($2/3$ cup) natural yoghurt

For the filling and topping

Chocolate Nut Frosting (see page 116)

Chocolate Nut Frosting

This is a delicious creamy icing that can be used in various light cakes and sponges.
This quantity gives a generous topping and filling
for the Chocolate Cake on page 115.

6 oz/175 g (6 squares) plain
(semi-sweet) chocolate

1/4 teaspoon vanilla essence
(extract)

1/4 pint/150 ml (2/3 cup)
double (heavy) cream

3 oz/75 g (2/3 cup) icing
(confectioners') sugar, sifted

3 oz/75 g (1/3 cup) pecan nuts
or walnuts, finely chopped

Break the chocolate into pieces. Melt in a basin set over a saucepan of hot water or in a microwave cooker. Leave to cool, but use it while still soft. Add the vanilla essence to the cream; whip lightly then blend into the chocolate with the sugar and nuts.

'A teapot should have a pleasing, well-balanced, compact shape,
capable of being cleaned inside and out; a lid that does not drop into the teacup;
a spout that does not soil the tablecloth, a handle that is both
safe and comfortable to hold and a knob that will not slip through the fingers.

If a teapot possesses these simple attributes,
then it justifies its existence, is a pleasure to use, and a credit to the manufacturers.'

Eric Owen, Wedgwood's chief-modeller for 20 years

Brazil Nut Loaf

Brazil nuts give a particular flavour
to baking which blends well with the dates in this sweet teabread.
Choose good-quality dessert dates that are moist.

Put the dates into a bowl, add the boiling water and stir well. Leave to stand until cold. Grease and flour a 2¹/₂ lb/1.2 kg loaf tin (pan). If the tin is inclined to stick, line it with greased greaseproof (wax) paper. Preheat the oven to 350F/180C/Gas Mark 4.

Rub the butter or margarine into the flour, or flour and baking powder. Add the sugar. Stir the eggs into the flour mixture with the dates, any liquid left from soaking these and the milk and Brazil nuts.

Beat briskly to blend and spoon the mixture into the prepared tin. Bake for approximately 55 minutes-1 hour, or until brown and firm. Allow to cool for 10 minutes before turning out of the tin. This loaf is better if left for at least 24 hours before cutting.

Slice fairly thickly and spread with butter, or as a pleasant change, soft cream cheese.

The Modern Touch

For added fibre, use wholemeal flour. In this case increase the amount of milk to 4 tablespoons (5 tbsp), and increase the cooking time by 5-10 minutes.

Alternatively, use 2 oz/50 g (scant ¹/₂ cup) rolled oats and 10 oz/ 300 g (2¹/₂ cups) flour. Sift an extra ¹/₂ teaspoon baking powder into the plain (all-purpose) flour or add this to self-raising flour, if using, to compensate for the weight of the rolled oats.

Makes 1 loaf

12 oz/350 g (2 cups) dates, stoned weight, coarsely chopped

¹/₄ pint/150 ml (²/₃ cup) boiling water

2 oz/50 g (¹/₄ cup) butter or margarine

12 oz/350 g (3 cups) self-raising flour or plain (all-purpose) flour sifted with 3 teaspoons baking powder

2 oz/50 g (¹/₄ cup) granulated or caster sugar

2 eggs, beaten

3 tablespoons (4 tbsp) milk

6 oz/175 g (1¹/₂ cups) Brazil nuts, coarsely chopped

Orange Chiffon Cake

The close links between Canada and the USA
are reflected in this light-as-a-feather Chiffon Cake. The use of corn oil
is a reminder of the importance and popularity of corn (maize) in North America.

Serves 8

8 oz/225 g (2 cups) self-raising
flour or plain (all-purpose)
flour sifted with 2 teaspoons
baking powder

8 oz/225 g (1 cup) caster
(granulated) sugar

3 fl oz/100 ml ($^3/_8$ cup) corn
(maize) oil

4 eggs

$^1/_4$ pint/150 ml ($^2/_3$ cup)
orange juice

2 teaspoons grated orange rind

2 extra egg whites

pinch cream of tartar

For the topping

1-2 oz/25-50 g ($^1/_4$-$^1/_2$ cup)
icing (confectioners') sugar,
sifted

Use a 9-10 inch/23-25 cm ungreased deep ring tin (tube pan). Heat the oven to 325F/160C/Gas Mark 3.

Sift the flour, or flour and baking powder, into a mixing bowl and add the sugar. Make a well in the centre and pour in the oil. Separate the eggs. Add the egg yolks, orange juice and rind to the oil. Beat the mixture with a spoon, or an electric mixer on a low speed, to form a smooth batter. If using a food processor, allow just 30 seconds.

Put the 6 egg whites into a dry bowl, add the cream of tartar and whisk until very stiff. Pour the orange batter on to the egg whites; gently fold the ingredients together until just blended then spoon into the tin.

Bake for 55 minutes, or until the cake is firm to a gentle touch. Invert the tin on to a wire cooling tray, but do not shake the cake. Leave until the cake falls out - this can take some minutes. When the cake is cold, dust liberally with icing sugar.

To Make a Change

Fill the centre of the ring with whipped cream and fresh strawberries and/or raspberries, or simply fill the centre with strings of redcurrants.

Butterscotch Cookies

These deliciously sweet biscuits have the flavour of dried apricots,
the tang of lemon and the goodness of rolled oats. Use the tenderized apricots
if you can get them.

Grease two baking (cookie) sheets or trays. Chop the apricots very finely (a food processor is ideal). Heat the butter and sugar in a bowl set over hot water until melted; beat in the apricots and lemon rind, blending well. Leave to cool.

Heat the oven to 325F/160C/Gas Mark 3.

Add the flour, or flour and baking powder, and oats to the apricot mixture. Knead well and roll into 20 balls. Place on the prepared sheets or trays and flatten gently with a fork. Bake for 10 minutes, or until crisp and pale golden. Cool slightly, then remove from the sheets or trays.

Store on their own in an airtight tin.

Makes 20

3 oz/75 g (1/2 cup) dried apricots

3 oz/75 g (3/8 cup) butter

3 oz/75 g (scant 3/8 cup) soft brown sugar

1 level teaspoon finely grated lemon rind

3 oz/75 g (3/4 cup) self-raising flour or plain (ali-purpose) flour sifted with 1 teaspoon baking powder

1 oz/25 g (scant 1/4 cup) rolled oats

Praline Puffs

French Canadians will certainly be familiar with choux pastry,
upon which these cakes are based. Choux pastry is best eaten the day it is made.

Makes 12

For the choux pastry

1/4 pint/150 ml (2/3 cup) water

2 oz/50 g (1/4 cup) butter or margarine

21/2 oz/65 g (1/2 cup plus 2 tbsp) plain (all-purpose) flour, well sifted with a pinch of salt

2 eggs, size 5 or 6 (medium)

For the filling and topping

4 oz/100 g (1/4 lb) praline or brittle nut toffee

1/4 pint/150 ml (2/3 cup) double (heavy) cream

a little icing (confectioners') sugar, sifted

1 teaspoon rum or brandy

Put the water and butter or margarine into a saucepan and heat gently until the butter or margarine has melted. Bring quickly to the boil, remove from the heat and add the flour all at once. Return to a low heat, beat until the mixture forms a ball and leaves the sides of the pan. Allow to cool.

Meanwhile grease a baking (cookie) sheet or tray and preheat the oven to 375-400F/190-200C/Gas Mark 5-6. Choose the higher setting, unless your oven is fierce.

Whisk the eggs lightly then gradually beat into the flour mixture until it has the consistency of a thick cream.

Spoon or pipe 12 rounds of the choux pastry on to the prepared baking sheet or tray. Bake for 20-25 minutes or until well risen, golden and really firm. Lift off the sheet and cool away from draughts. Slit the buns to allow the steam to escape; if there is a very small amount of uncooked mixture in the centre, remove with a spoon.

Place the praline or toffee between sheets of greaseproof (wax) paper and crush with a rolling pin. Whip the cream. Add the crushed praline, or toffee, 1 or 2 teaspoons of icing sugar and the rum or brandy.

Insert a generous amount of the cream mixture in each puff. To decorate, sprinkle with icing sugar.

Anzacs

These biscuits (cookies) are beautifully crisp and the combination of coconut and rolled oats gives a particularly interesting flavour.
They are popular in Australia as well as New Zealand, as the name indicates.
Anzacs was the name given to the Australian and New Zealand Army Forces who served in the First and Second World Wars.

Grease 2 or 3 flat baking (cookie) sheets or trays. Heat the oven to 325F/160C/Gas Mark 3.

Cream the butter or margarine with the sugar and golden syrup. Add the flour and baking powder, coconut and rolled oats, mixing well.

Roll the dough into small balls with slightly dampened fingers. Place them on the prepared baking sheet or trays, allowing space for the mixture to spread in cooking. Press a halved cherry on top of each ball. Bake for 15-20 minutes until golden brown. Leave to cool for 5 minutes before transferring to a wire tray.

Store on their own in an airtight tin.

Makes 24-30

4 oz/100 g (1/2 cup) butter or margarine

4 oz/100 g (1/2 cup) caster (granulated) sugar

1 tablespoon (1 1/4 tbsp) golden (light corn) syrup

4 oz/110 g (1 cup) plain (all-purpose) flour sifted with 1/2 teaspoon baking powder

4 oz/110 g (1 1/4 cups) desiccated (shredded) coconut

4 oz/110 g (scant cup) rolled oats

To decorate

12-15 glacé candied cherries, halved

Crystallized Fruit Cake

This rich cake needs some days to mature after baking. Store in an airtight tin.
It has a delicious and unusual combination of flavours.

Serves 12-16

4 oz/100 g (2/3 cup) dried apricots, finely diced

4 tablespoons (5 tbsp) sweet sherry

10 oz/300 g (1 1/4 cups) butter

10 oz/300 g (1 1/2 cups) caster (granulated) sugar

1 teaspoon finely grated lemon rind

2 teaspoons finely grated orange rind

1 tablespoon (1 1/4 tbsp) golden (light corn) syrup

5 eggs, size 1 or 2 (jumbo)

10 oz/300 g (2 1/2 cups) plain (all-purpose) flour

50 g/2 oz (1/2 cup) ground almonds

6 oz/175 g (1 cup) candied peel, finely chopped

4 oz/100 g (2/3 cup) angelica, finely chopped

6 oz/175 g (1 cup) glacé (candied) cherries, quartered

6 oz/175 g (1 cup) crystallized (candied) pineapple, diced

4 oz/100 g (2/3 cup) crystallized (candied) apricots, finely diced

4 oz/100 g (1 cup) almonds, blanched and chopped

8 oz/225 g (1 1/3 cups) sultanas

Soak the apricots in the sherry for 3 hours. Line a 9 inch/23 cm round cake tin (pan) first with thick brown paper and then greased greaseproof (wax) paper. Heat the oven to 325F/160C/Gas Mark 3.

Cream the butter, sugar, fruit rinds and syrup until soft and light. Beat in the eggs one by one; add the flour and ground almonds, the apricots with any sherry not absorbed by these and the rest of the ingredients. Mix very thoroughly. Spoon into the prepared tin.

Place in the oven and bake for 1 hour. Reduce the temperature to 275-300F/140-150C/Gas Mark 1-2. Use the lower setting if your oven is inclined to be fierce and bake for a further 1 3/4-2 hours or until the cake is firm to the touch. Listen carefully: if the cake is not adequately cooked it gives a humming sound. If cooked, it is silent. Allow to cool completely in the baking tin before turning out.

To Make a Change

Top with sieved apricot jam (jelly) and neatly diced crystallized fruits.

Coconut Fruit Cake

The addition of coconut adds an unexpected flavour
and texture to a light fruit cake. Allow enough time for the coconut to soak
in the orange juice and sherry before preparing the cake.

Soak the coconut and peel in the orange juice and sherry for 1-2 hours.

Line the base of a 7 1/2 inch/19 cm tin (pan) with greased greaseproof (wax) paper; grease and flour the sides of the tin. Heat the oven to 325F/160C/Gas Mark 3.

Cream the butter or margarine and sugar until soft and light. Gradually beat in the eggs. Add the flour, or flour and baking powder, the softened coconut and peel, cherries and sultanas.

Spoon into the prepared tin and bake for 1 1/2 hours or until firm and golden brown. Cool for 5 minutes in the tin then turn out carefully on to a wire tray, to cool completely.

Serves 8-10

4 oz/100 g (1 1/4 cups) desiccated (shredded) coconut

4 oz/100 g (2/3 cup) candied peel, finely chopped

4 tablespoons (5 tbsp) orange juice

2 tablespoons (2 1/2 tbsp) sweet sherry

5 oz/150 g (5/8 cup) butter or margarine

5 oz/150 g (5/8 cup) caster (granulated) sugar

3 eggs, size 1 or 2 (jumbo)

6 oz/175 g (1 1/2 cups) self-raising flour or plain (all-purpose) flour sifted with 1 1/2 teaspoons baking powder

3 oz/75 g (3/8 cup) glacé (candied) cherries, quartered

8 oz/225 g (1 1/4 cups) sultanas (seedless white raisins)

Banana Loaf

This moist loaf has a wonderfully rich and
sweet flavour and nutty texture, but does not rise dramatically in baking.
It is best stored for 24 hours before cutting.

Makes 1 loaf

2 oz/50 g (¼ cup) butter or
margarine

2 oz/50 g (¼ cup) caster
(granulated) sugar

2 eggs

8 oz/225 g (2 cups) self-raising
flour or plain (all-purpose)
flour sifted with 2 teaspoons
baking powder

½ teaspoon bicarbonate of
soda (baking soda)

2 large bananas

6 fl oz/175 ml (¾ cup) natural
yoghurt

2 oz/50 g (⅓ cup) sultanas
(seedless white raisins)

2 oz/50 g (½ cup) finely
grated carrots (weight when
grated)

2 oz/50 g (⅓ cup) pecan nuts
or walnuts, coarsely chopped

To decorate

A few pecan nuts or walnut
halves

Grease and flour or line a 2 lb/900 g (2 lb) loaf tin (pan) with greased greaseproof (wax) paper. Heat the oven to 350F/180C/Gas Mark 4.

Cream the butter or margarine with the sugar until soft and light. Whisk the eggs well; sift the flour, or flour and baking powder, with the bicarbonate of soda. Slice, then mash the bananas with the yoghurt. Blend the eggs, flour and banana and yoghurt into the creamed mixture. Stir in the dried fruit, grated carrot and nuts and mix thoroughly.

Spoon the mixture into the prepared tin and smooth the top. Arrange the nuts on the surface in a neat design. Bake for 1 hour, or until firm to the touch. Leave to cool in the tin for 5-10 minutes, then turn out to cool completely.

The Modern Touch

Use half white flour and half wholemeal (wholewheat) flour to increase the fibre content of the loaf.

Hermits

Hermit is a name that describes a range of cookies popular in North America,
but I first enjoyed this version in South Africa,
so it seems they have an international following. If the dough is slightly soft,
chill it for up to 30 minutes before rolling it out.

Heat the oven to 375F/190C/Gas Mark 5.

Sift the flour and spices together. Cream the butter or margarine and sugar. Beat in the egg. Fold in the flour and add the remaining ingredients. Knead the dough well; roll out to a thickness of 14 inch/6 mm and cut into rounds. Arrange on the baking sheets or trays and bake for 12 minutes, or until firm. Allow to cool on the baking sheets or trays.

To Make a Change
American Hermit Drop Cookies. Use 6 oz/175 g (1 1/2 cups) self-raising flour or add 1 1/2 teaspoons baking powder to the plain (all-purpose) flour in the recipe above. Add a second egg and 4 tablespoons (5 tbsp) milk to give a batter-like consistency. Drop from a teaspoon on to the greased baking sheets or trays to give about 24-30 little rounds.

Bake at 375F/190C/Gas Mark 5 for 15 minutes or until firm to the touch for soft cookies. If you prefer a slightly crisper texture cook for 5 minutes more, reducing the heat slightly. Remove carefully while warm.

These soft cookies must be stored in an airtight tin away from crisp biscuits, although they are nicest eaten soon after baking.

Makes approximately 24

6 oz/175 g (3/4 cup) plain (all-purpose) flour

1/2 teaspoon ground cinnamon

1/2 teaspoon ground ginger

4 oz/110 g (1/2 cup) butter or margarine

4 oz/110 g (scant 1/2 cup) brown sugar

1 egg

2 oz/50 g (1/3 cup) currants or chopped raisins

2 oz/50 g (1/3 cup) walnuts, finely chopped

1 oz/25 g (1/3 cup) desiccated (shredded) coconut

Koeksisters

These deep-fried cakes are coated with a well-spiced
syrup and are delicious for teatime. Make the syrup ahead so it can cool.
Eat these cakes when freshly made.

Makes 12-18

For the syrup

1 lb/450 g (2 1/2 cups) caster or
granulated sugar

1/2 pint/300 ml (1 1/4 cups)
water

2 inch/5 cm cinnamon stick or 1
piece fresh ginger, well
bruised

1/2 teaspoon grated lemon rind

2 teaspoons lemon juice

For the cake

10 oz/300 g (2 1/2 cups) self-
raising flour sifted with 1 level
teaspoon baking powder or
plain (all-purpose) flour sifted
with 3 level teaspoons baking
powder

a pinch of salt

1 1/2 oz/40 g (3 tbsp) butter or
margarine

1 tablespoon (1 1/4 tbsp) caster
(granulated) sugar

1 egg, beaten water to bind oil
for frying

Put all the syrup ingredients in a saucepan. Stir over a low heat until the sugar has dissolved, then simmer gently for 2-3 minutes. Allow to cool, then refrigerate until ready to use.

Sift the flour, baking powder and salt together. Rub in the butter or margarine and add the sugar. Stir in half the egg, reserving the remainder to seal the ends of the cakes. Mix well. Gradually add enough water to make a soft rolling consistency. Cover and chill for 30 minutes. Roll out the dough until 1/4 inch/6 mm in thickness and cut into 36 strips each 1/4 inch/6 mm wide and 3-3 1/2 inches/7.5-8.5 cm long. Plait 3 strips together for larger cakes; use 2 strips for narrower cakes. Press the ends together very firmly and seal with a little beaten egg.

Heat the oil to 375F/190C and fry the cakes for 1-2 minutes until golden brown. Lift out with a perforated spoon and immediately dip into the cold syrup. Place on a wire cooling tray, with a dish underneath to catch any drips. Leave to dry for 1 hour.

Peach Meringue Gâteau

South Africa grows an abundance of fruit, and the recipe that follows
makes use of fresh peaches. When they are out of season,
use canned fruit, well drained. Van der Hum liqueur is very popular in South Africa
and contains, among other things, brandy, rum, spices and orange blossom.

Grease a baking (cookie) sheet or tray. Heat the oven to 300F/150C/Gas Mark 2.

Cream the butter and sugar until soft. Beat in the egg yolk and fold in the ground almonds and flour. Knead well and press or roll into a neat 9 inch/23 cm round on the prepared baking (cookie) sheet or tray. Prick the shortbread neatly all over with a fine skewer and bake for 20-25 minutes, or until it starts to become firm. Remove from the oven. Reduce the temperature to 275F/140C/Gas Mark 1, then prepare the meringue.

To make the meringue, whisk the egg white until stiff and gradually beat in the sugar. Spoon or pipe a narrow border or rosettes of meringue around the edge of the shortbread. Cook for 30 minutes then leave to cool. Transfer the shortbread to a serving plate.

Skin and halve the peaches and sprinkle with the brandy, rum or liqueur and the sugar. Carefully spread the shortbread with the jam. Whip the cream and spread it over the jam. Top with the peaches, rounded side uppermost. The peaches should be prepared at the last minute.

Serves 8

For the shortbread base

4 oz/110 g (1/2 cup) butter

3 oz/75 g (3/8 cup) caster (granulated) sugar

1 egg yolk

1 oz/25 g (1/4 cup) ground almonds

4 oz/110 g (1 cup) plain (all-purpose) flour

For the meringue

1 egg white

2 oz/50 g (1/4 cup) caster (granulated) sugar

For the filling

4 ripe peaches

1 tablespoon (1 1/4 tbsp) brandy, rum or Van der Hum liqueur

1 tablespoon (1 1/4 tbsp) caster (granulated) sugar

2 tablespoons (2 1/2 tbsp) peach or apricot jam (jelly)

1/4 pint/150 ml (2/3 cup) double (heavy) cream

Cranberry Loaf

Cranberries, which figure in many American recipes,
may well have been known originally as 'crane berries', since cranes showed
a distinct liking for them. The dark red berries have a
distinctive bloom and a sharp flavour. If using frozen cranberries, chop them
before they are completely thawed, or they will be too soft.

Makes 1 loaf

8 oz/225 g (2 cups) plain (all-purpose) flour

1 1/2 teaspoons baking powder

1/2 teaspoon bicarbonate of soda (baking soda)

a pinch of salt

6 oz/175 g (3/4 cup) caster (granulated) sugar

4 oz/100 g (1 cup) raw cranberries, roughly chopped

2 teaspoons grated orange rind

6 fl oz/175 ml (3/4 cup) orange juice

1 1/2 oz/40 g (3 tbsp) butter or margarine, melted

1 egg

2 oz/50 g (1/3 cup) seedless raisins

2 oz/50 g (1/2 cup) pecan nuts or walnuts, coarsely chopped

Line a 2-2 1/2 lb/900 g-1.2 kg loaf tin (pan) with well-greased greaseproof (wax) paper. This is very important, since this mixture is inclined to stick to the tin. Heat the oven to 325F/160C/Gas Mark 3.

Sift the flour, baking powder, bicarbonate of soda and salt together. Add the sugar, the chopped cranberries and the rest of the ingredients. Combine thoroughly, then spoon the mixture into the prepared tin.

Bake for 1 hour and 5 minutes, or until firm to the touch. Cool for 10 minutes in the tin, then carefully turn out on to a wire tray. Remove the paper while the loaf is just warm. If it shows signs of sticking to the loaf, brush with a little cold water.

Make this loaf a day before it is required, since it is very crumbly when fresh.

Devil's Food Cake

In this mocha version of Devil's Food Cake the blend of coffee and chocolate gives it a sophisticated flavour.

Break the chocolate into pieces and place in a bowl. Add the coffee and set the bowl over hot water until the chocolate melts or use the microwave cooker. Allow to cool.

Line the base of two 9 inch/23 cm sandwich tins (layer pans) with greased greaseproof (wax) paper. Grease the sides of the tins well. Heat the oven to 350F/180C/Gas Mark 4.

Cream the butter or margarine with the sugar and vanilla essence. Separate the eggs and beat the yolks into the creamed mixture. Sift the flour, or flour and baking powder, with the bicarbonate of soda. Blend into the mixture, together with the chocolate-flavoured coffee, and add the yoghurt, or soured cream or milk. Mix thoroughly.

Whisk the egg whites until just stiff then fold into the soft batter. Spoon the mixture into the prepared tins. Bake for 25 minutes or until firm to the touch. Cool in the tins for 2 or 3 minutes then turn out on to a wire tray to cool completely.

Make up the white frosting and use half to sandwich the 2 layers together. Coat the top and sides of the cake with the remainder. Place the chocolate in a bowl set over hot water to melt. Cool slightly and, using a teaspoon, trickle the chocolate spiral fashion over the top of the cake.

Serves 6-8

3 oz/85 g (3 squares) plain (semi-sweet) chocolate

4 fl oz/120 ml (1/2 cup) strong hot coffee

3 oz/85 g (3/8 cup) butter or margarine

8 oz/225 g (1 cup) caster (granulated) sugar

1/2 teaspoon vanilla essence (extract)

3 eggs

8 oz/225 g (2 cups) self-raising flour or plain (all-purpose) flour sifted with 2 teaspoons baking powder

1/2 teaspoon bicarbonate of soda (baking soda)

4 fl oz/120 ml (1/2 cup) yoghurt or soured cream or fresh milk plus 1/2 teaspoon cream of tartar

To decorate

Frosting made with 12 oz/350 g (1 1/2 cups) sugar (see page 130)

2 oz/50 g (2 squares) plain (semi-sweet) chocolate

Lady Baltimore Cake

This cake was created by an American belle and inspired the title of a book by Owen Wister, published in 1906. Since that time it has become one of the best-known American cakes. The recipes vary, but all are based on egg whites.

Serves 8-10

12 oz/350 g (3 cups) self-raising flour sifted with 3 level teaspoons baking powder or plain (all-purpose) flour sifted with 6 level teaspoons baking powder

a pinch of salt

6 oz/175 g (³/4 cup) white cooking fat (shortening)

12 oz/350 g (1¹/2 cups) caster (granulated) sugar

¹/2 teaspoon vanilla essence (extract)

8 fl oz/225 ml (1 cup) milk or milk and water

6 egg whites

For the frosting

12 oz/350 g (1¹/2 cups) caster or granulated sugar

4 fl oz/110 ml (¹/2 cup) water

scant 1 tablespoon (1 tbsp) golden (light corn) syrup

2 egg whites

¹/2 teaspoon vanilla essence (extract)

Line the base of three 9 inch/23 cm sandwich tins (layer pans) with greased greaseproof (wax) paper; grease and flour the sides. Heat the oven to 375F/190C/Gas Mark 5. If your oven is inclined to be on the fierce side, heat to 350F/180C/Gas Mark 4.

Sift the flour, baking powder and salt together twice. Cream the fat with half the sugar and vanilla essence until soft and light. Beat a little milk into the mixture, then add a little flour. Continue in this way until all the milk and flour are blended with the creamed mixture.

Whisk the egg whites in another bowl until stiff, but not overdry. Fold in the remaining sugar. Take about a third of the egg whites and beat into the creamed mixture to give it a softer texture. Fold in the remaining egg whites gently, but thoroughly.

Divide the mixture between the tins. Bake for 20 minutes at the higher setting, or 25 at the lower one, or until firm to a gentle touch. Cool for 5 minutes in the tins then turn out carefully on to a wire tray. Remove the lining paper and leave to become quite cold.

To make the frosting, put the sugar, water and syrup into a heavy saucepan. Stir over a low heat until the sugar dissolves. Cover the pan and boil steadily for 3 minutes (this prevents the mixture crystallizing). Remove the lid and boil steadily until the mixture reaches 238-240F/114-115C on a sugar thermometer or forms a soft ball when tested in cold water. While the syrup is boiling, whisk the egg whites until stiff. Pour the hot syrup in a steady stream over the egg whites, beating vigorously until the mixture thickens. Add the vanilla essence. Blend just under half the frosting with the filling ingredients and use to sandwich the layers together. Coat the top and sides of the cake with the remaining frosting.

To Make a Change

The basic cake is known as a white, a snow or even a silver cake: the white fat keeps it light in colour, but butter could be used instead.

The nuts and fruits can be soaked in brandy overnight before blending with the filling.

In the frosting you can omit the golden syrup and add a pinch of cream of tartar to the mixture when the syrup is poured on to the egg whites.

Lord Baltimore Cake. Use the recipe for Lady Baltimore Cake, but substitute 6 egg yolks for the 6 egg whites. Omit the golden syrup in the frosting and substitute 2 tablespoons (2^1/$_2$ tbsp) lemon juice for 2 tablespoons (2^1/$_2$ tbsp) of the water. When the frosting has stiffened blend just under half with 2 tablespoons (2^1/$_2$ tbsp) chopped maraschino cherries, 3 oz/75 g (^{1}/$_2$ cup) blanched and lightly toasted chopped almonds, and 3 oz/75 g (1 cup) browned desiccated (shredded) coconut. Use the remaining frosting to coat the cake.

For the filling

2 oz/50 g (^{1}/$_2$ cup) almonds, blanched and chopped

3 oz/75 g (^{3}/$_4$ cup) pecan nuts or walnuts, chopped

3 oz/75 g (^{1}/$_2$ cup) seedless raisins

2 fresh or dried figs, finely diced

Pineapple Cheesecake

Americans love cheesecake, and the refreshing pineapple and lemon flavour
of this one makes it good enough to serve as a dessert.

Serves 6-8

For the base

6 oz/175 g (1 1/2 cups)
digestive biscuits (Graham
crackers), crushed

2 oz/50 g (1/4 cup) butter,
melted

1 oz/25 g (2 tbsp) caster
(granulated) sugar

For the topping

one 1 lb/453 g can pineapple
rings in syrup

1 lb/450 g (2 cups) cream or
curd cheese

2 oz/50 g (1/4 cup) butter

2 oz/50 g (1/4 cup) caster
(granulated) sugar

1 teaspoon finely grated lemon
rind

3 eggs

1 oz/25 g (scant 1/4 cup)
cornflour (cornstarch)

1 tablespoon (1 1/4 tbsp) lemon
juice

3 tablespoons (4 tbsp) double
(heavy) cream

For the glaze and decoration

1 tablespoon (1 1/4 tbsp) lemon
juice

1/4 pint/150 ml (2/3 cup)
pineapple syrup

1 1/2 level teaspoons arrowroot

whipped cream

Grease a 9 inch/23 cm springform tin (pan) or cake tin (pan) with a
loose base. Heat the oven to 300F/150C/Gas Mark 2.

Combine the biscuit crumbs evenly with the butter and sugar. Press
into the bottom of the tin. Drain and chop the pineapple, reserving 3
rings for decoration. Thoroughly blend together the cheese, butter,
sugar and lemon rind. Separate the eggs. Add the yolks to the cheese
mixture and fold in the cornflour. Add the lemon juice, chopped
pineapple and cream. Mix well. Whisk the egg whites and fold them
gently into the mixture.

Spoon the filling into the tin. Bake for 1 1/4 hours or until just firm.
Turn off the heat and cool the cheesecake in the oven with the door
ajar. This prevents the top wrinkling.

For the glaze, blend the lemon juice, pineapple syrup and arrowroot.
Pour into a saucepan set over a moderate heat. Stir until thickened,
then leave to cool. Cut the reserved pineapple rings in neat portions
and arrange on the cheesecake. Brush the top with the glaze and
decorate with cream.

Ice Box Cookies

These American cookies, which might well
be called Refrigerator Cookies in these modern days, are given their name
because the dough is chilled before cutting.

Cream the butter or margarine and vanilla sugar, or sugar and vanilla essence. Add the flour and mix well. Form the dough into a neat roll. If it is too soft, wrap and chill for a short time before shaping. Wrap the roll and leave in the refrigerator until firm enough to slice. Meanwhile, heat the oven to 325F/160C/Gas Mark 3.

Unwrap the biscuit dough and cut it into thin slices with a sharp knife. Place the slices on ungreased baking (cookie) sheets or trays and bake for 12-15 minutes. Cool on a wire tray. When completely cold, store in an airtight tin.

To Make a Change
Chocolate Cookies. Substitute 1 oz/25 g (1/4 cup) chocolate powder for the same weight of flour. When the cookies are cold, top with melted chocolate.

Makes 20-30

6 oz/175 g (3/4 cup) butter or margarine

4 oz/110 g (1/2 cup) vanilla sugar or caster (granulated) sugar plus 1/2 teaspoon vanilla essence (extract)

8 oz/225 g (2 cups) plain (all-purpose) flour

Come, little cottage girl, you seem
To want my cup of tea;
And will you take a little cream?
Now tell the truth to me.

Barry Pain (1864-1928)

High Tea

———

High tea is a uniquely British meal; it allows you to enjoy
a pleasant mixture of savoury and sweet ingredients, with a generous quantity
of tea to drink. High teas are mentioned by Mrs Beeton,
who, well over a hundred years ago, stated that:

'High tea is a permanent institution, quite taking the place of late supper;
young people preferring it to dinner. It being a
movable feast that can be partaken of at hours that will not interfere
with tennis, boating and other amusements and but little formality is needed.'

The high tea menus of the nineteenth century might well have included
1 or 2 hot dishes, cold chicken, game, tongue, ham and salad.
There would be homemade bread, scones, a selection of cakes and cold fruit tarts
with cream. Tea would accompany this marvellous array of satisfying food.

High tea is still a popular meal in many parts of Britain, particularly
Scotland, Ireland, parts of Wales and the North of England, especially Yorkshire.
It is ideal for a family with children since it generally is served
between 5 and 7 pm. In Scotland you may well find hotels that offer a high tea
as well as dinner, so guests can choose the meal they prefer.

Modern High Teas

There are no rules about what is correct for high tea. The savoury dish, hot or cold, is generally served first and followed by scones, or bread and butter, with jam (jelly), cake, biscuits (cookies), fruit tarts or other sweet fare. Fruit salad and cream is not unknown for high tea.

The famous British breakfast of bacon and eggs is just as likely to appear on the tea table. You may be fortunate enough to be offered this dish on a farm where both the bacon and the eggs are home-produced. Fish and chips (French fries) are another established favourite with young and old.

Sandwiches may well be part of the menu, for good bread is now considered to be a very important food, since it contributes carbohydrate and fibre to the diet. There are suggestions for sandwiches on page 67. Remember that the sandwiches included in a satisfying high tea should be more substantial than those offered for afternoon tea.

Salads

Now that everyone knows the importance of including fibre in a balanced diet, a modern high tea may well feature a variety of salad ingredients. The salad could be served with cooked meats, a pasty, cold poached salmon or tuna fish or with hard-boiled eggs, which are generally coated with mayonnaise. Cheese salads are very popular and look particularly appetizing if more than one kind of cheese is used. Grate the cheese fairly coarsely, or cut it into slices, arranged centrally with a border of colourful salad. Since fruit blends well with cheese, the salad could include segments of orange, rings of cored, but not peeled, dessert apple coated with mayonnaise or sprinkled with lemon juice to prevent discoloration, canned or fresh pineapple slices or dried fruit such as dates or raisins.

Toasted Snacks

Poached or scrambled eggs on toast are quickly prepared for high tea, and are filling and nutritious. Cheese on toast is a popular savoury: simply place slices of cheese or grated cheese over hot buttered toast and place under a preheated grill. Leave for a short time until the cheese melts. Serve at once, topped with sliced or grilled tomatoes. The recipe for a classic Welsh Rarebit is on page 144.

Baked beans on toast have always been a favourite with children. In the past parents often felt this was very uninteresting, but nowadays beans have won universal approval because of their high fibre content. The beans can be heated in a saucepan or in a covered container in a microwave cooker.

Sardines, cooked mushrooms and halved tomatoes on toast are other easy dishes for high tea.

Fish and Chips

Many adults and children would list fried fish and chips (French fries)
as their favourite hot dish for any meal, including high tea.

Serves 4

4 portions of white fish, such as
cod, haddock or plaice
(flounder)

1 tablespoon (1 1/4 tbsp) flour

salt and pepper

1 egg

2 oz/50 g (1/2 cup) fine crisp
breadcrumbs

approximately 1 lb/450 g (1 lb)
potatoes

oil or fat, for frying

To garnish

lemon wedges or slices

Dry the fish well on absorbent kitchen paper. Place the flour on a
plate and season lightly with salt and pepper. Dust the fish portions
all over with flour. This helps the egg and breadcrumb coating adhere
to the fish.

Beat the egg well on a deep plate and dip in the fish portions until
they are well covered on all sides. Place the breadcrumbs on another
plate and use to coat the fish. Press the crumbs firmly to the fish and
shake off any surplus.

Cut the potatoes into chip (finger) shapes or slices and keep in cold
water until ready to fry for the first time. Double frying the potatoes
ensures that they are beautifully crisp.

Heat the oil or fat to a temperature of 340F/170C or until a cube of
day-old bread turns golden brown within 1 minute, but no quicker.
Cook the potatoes in batches. Dry some on absorbent kitchen paper.
Place the first batch into a frying basket, if you are using one, or
directly into the fat. Fry for 5-6 minutes or until tender, but still pale in
colour. Remove, shaking off any surplus fat or oil over the pan. Leave
on a dish while cooking the remaining potatoes, in the same way.
When all the potatoes are cooked, place the prepared fish in the oil
and fry until tender. Place the portions on a heated dish and keep hot.

Reheat the oil or fat to a temperature of 375F/190C or until a cube of
bread turns golden in 30 seconds. Add the potatoes and fry for 1-2
minutes, or until crisp and brown. Drain the potatoes over the pan of
oil and place on absorbent kitchen paper to drain completely.
Transfer the fish and fried potatoes to individual plates and garnish
with lemon.

Cornish Pasties

These savoury pastries are equally good for a high tea or a packed meal and they have always been part of the fare carried by Cornish miners.

Lightly grease a baking (cookie) sheet or tray. Heat the oven to 425F/220C/Gas Mark 7.

Sift the flour and salt into a mixing bowl. Rub in the fat until the mixture resembles fine breadcrumbs. Add enough cold water to give a firm rolling consistency. Roll out the pastry on a floured surface to a 1/4 inch/6 mm thickness. Either cut it into 4-6 rounds (the latter size is generally ideal for teatime) or form into a large round for a family-size pasty.

Mix the filling ingredients together. Place a little of the filling in the centre of each pastry round. Dampen the edges and bring them together, making a firm seal. Flute the edges, forming 4 or 6 upright pasties or one large pasty. Beat the egg with the water and brush over the pastry to glaze.

Place on the prepared sheet and bake for 20 minutes; reduce the heat to 325F/160C/Gas Mark 3 and bake the smaller pasties for a further 25-30 minutes or allow a further 45 minutes for a single large pasty.

Serve hot or cold with a crisp green salad.

Serves 4-6

For the shortcrust pastry

12 oz/350 g (3 cups) plain (all-purpose) flour

pinch salt

6 oz/175 g (3/4 cup) fat (shortening) water to bind

For the filling

12 oz/350 g (3/4 lb) rump (boneless sirloin) steak, finely diced

2 medium potatoes, peeled and diced

2 medium onions, peeled and diced

salt and pepper

1 tablespoon (1 1/4 tbsp) stock or water

1 teaspoon chopped mixed fresh herbs

To glaze the pastry

1 egg

1 tablespoon (1 1/4 tbsp) water

Dublin Bay Prawns

These large prawns caught in Irish waters are a form of lobster that is plentiful
in the cold waters of northern Europe.
You will need about 8 oz/225 g prawns for each serving.

Dublin Bay prawns

butter

lemon juice

salt and pepper

It is usual to cook raw Dublin Bay prawns by steaming them over a
pan of boiling water. They take about 10 minutes, check carefully;
when the shells turn bright pink they are cooked. Alternatively the
raw shellfish can be simmered in water in a saucepan for about the
same time.

When the prawns are cold, remove the heads and shells. Heat a
generous knob of butter in a pan and add a little lemon juice and
seasoning. Turn the fish in this mixture for a few minutes, but do not
overheat or they will become tough. Serve with fresh bread and
butter.

Champ

This is a famous Irish dish which can be served at teatime
with fried or grilled bacon or with fried, poached or scrambled eggs.

Serves 4

1 bunch spring onions
   (scallions) or 2-3 leeks,
   cleaned and sliced

4 tablespoons (5 tbsp) milk

salt and pepper

1 lb/450 g (2 cups) smooth
   creamed potatoes

2 oz/50 g (4 tbsp) butter,
   melted

Add the spring onions (scallions) or leeks to the milk in a saucepan.
Season lightly, cover the pan and simmer for about 10 minutes. Add
the vegetables and any milk left in the saucepan to the potatoes and
beat well. Transfer to a heated serving dish. Make a well in the centre
and spoon in the hot melted butter.

Scots Herrings

This method of cooking fresh herrings, which are coated with oatmeal
(the modern rolled oats could be used)
gives the fish a lovely crisp coating which keeps in all the fine flavour of the herrings.

Split and clean the fish and remove the heads. Most fishmongers will do this for you. The herrings can be split and the backbones removed, and the fish opened out and served flat.

If cooking unboned fish, score them lightly with a knife along the side, making several shallow cuts. Season the oatmeal or rolled oats with salt and pepper and use to coat the fish, pressing the coating firmly into the flesh.

Heat the fat in a frying pan (skillet) set over a moderate heat. Fry the fish for about 10 minutes if whole, 7-8 minutes if opened out, turning once, until golden on both sides. Drain on absorbent kitchen paper and serve piping hot, garnished with parsley and lemon.

Serves 4

4 large fresh herrings

2 oz/50 g (1/3 cup) oatmeal or
the same weight (1/2 cup)
rolled oats

salt and pepper

2 oz/50 g (1/4 cup) fat
(shortening) for frying

To garnish

parsley sprigs

lemon wedges

'A hardened and shameless tea drinker, who has for many years
diluted his meals with only the infusion of this fascinating plant. Whose kettle
has scarcely time to cool; who with tea amuses the evening,
with tea solaces the midnights and with tea welcomes the morning.'

Dr Johnson (1709-1784) referring to himself in an article in the *Literary Magazine*

Arbroath Smokies

These fine fish, which are smoked whole,
and the more robust finnan haddie (haddock) are justly famous in Scotland.
They are ideal for a high tea.

Serves 4

4 Arbroath smokies

approximately 2 oz/50 g
  (¹/₄ cup) butter

freshly ground black pepper

Arbroath smokies have such a delicate texture that they need little cooking. Place the fish in a frying pan (skillet) on the hob or under a preheated grill (broiler) and cook for 1-2 minutes on each side. The fish is so tender that heating it like this is all that is necessary at this stage. Split the fish and open out flat. Spread with the butter and sprinkle with pepper. Close up the fish again and reheat for a few minutes only.

Serve with fresh bread or soft rolls, known as baps in Scotland.

Grilled Finnan Haddie

Finnan haddock is often poached in water or milk,
or a mixture of milk and water. In many parts of Britain the cooked drained fish
is topped with butter and a poached egg.

Serves 4

1 large or 2 smaller finnan
  haddock

1-2 oz/25-50 g (2-4
  tablespoons) butter, melted

4 bacon rashers

Preheat the grill (broiler).

Cut the tails and fins from the fish and divide into 4 portions. Brush with the butter. Place under the grill and cook the fish for about 3 minutes each side. After turning the fish, add the bacon rashers (slices) and grill until crisp. Serve each portion of haddock with a slice of bacon.

Anglesey Eggs

This is a very sustaining dish, ideal for people who take high tea instead of supper or dinner.
The combination of potatoes and leeks is typical of Welsh cooking.

Place the potatoes in a saucepan of boiling salted water and cook for 15 minutes. Hard-boil the eggs. Add the leeks and a little pepper to the potatoes and continue cooking until both vegetables are tender. Strain and mash with half the butter or margarine. Spoon the potatoes and leeks around the edge of a heatproof dish. Slice the hard-boiled eggs. Heat the oven to 375F/190C/Gas Mark 5.

Heat the remaining butter or margarine in a small saucepan. Stir in the flour and cook for 2 or 3 minutes, still stirring. Blend in the milk. Bring the sauce to the boil, stirring over the heat until it is thickened and smooth. Add three-quarters of the cheese, the sliced eggs and seasoning to taste. Spoon the sauce into the centre of the potato and leek ring and top with the remaining cheese.

Place in the oven and bake for 25-30 minutes. Serve hot, garnished with chopped parsley.

Note: If all the ingredients are hot you can use a flameproof dish and heat the completed dish under the grill.

Serves 4-6

1 lb/450 g (1 lb) potatoes

salt and pepper

4 or 6 eggs

12 oz/350 g (3/4 lb) leeks, thinly sliced

2 oz/50 g (1/4 cup) butter or margarine

1 oz/25 g (1/4 cup) plain (all-purpose) flour

1/2 pint/300 ml (1 1/4 cups) milk

3-4 oz/75-100 g (3/4-1 cup) Cheddar or Caerphilly cheese, grated or crumbled

To garnish

chopped parsley

Welsh Rarebit

Despite its name, this savoury dish is not exclusive to Wales,
but is served in most parts of Britain. It used to be served as a savoury at the end
of a meal, a habit beloved of Victorians. It is also excellent for high tea.
The type of cheese used varies. Double Gloucester has always been a great favourite
for this dish, but Cheshire, Cheddar or Lancashire
(which has to be crumbled rather than grated) are all ideal.

Serves 6

1 oz/25 g (2 tbsp) butter or margarine

1 oz/25 g (4 tbsp) plain (all-purpose) flour

4 tablespoons (5 tbsp) milk or single cream

3 tablespoons (4 tbsp) beer or ale

1-1 1/2 teaspoons made English or French mustard

12 oz-1 lb/350-450 g (3-4 cups) cheese, grated

salt and pepper

6 large slices of bread

a little softened butter, for spreading

To garnish

parsley sprigs

tomato slices

Heat the butter or margarine in a saucepan. Stir in the flour and cook gently for 1 or 2 minutes. Add the milk or cream and the beer or ale. Stir or whisk vigorously. This sauce becomes very thick and must be smooth. Add the mustard and cheese then salt and pepper to taste. It is advisable to add salt and pepper after the cheese, for the salt content varies considerably. Remove the pan from the heat.

Preheat the grill (broiler). Toast the slices of bread and spread thinly with butter. Divide the cheese mixture between the slices of toast. Place under the preheated grill and cook until golden in colour and bubbling. Serve hot, garnished with parsley and tomato.

To Make a Change

Buck Rarebit. While the cheese is heating on the toast, poach 1 egg per portion and drain well. Place on the hot cheese and serve at once.

York Rarebit. Top the hot buttered toast with slices of cooked York ham. Cover the ham with the Rarebit mixture and cook as above.

Potted Salmon

Potted foods have been popular throughout Britain for generations.
Now that commercially potted fish and various meats are generally available they
are less often prepared at home. These suggestions are ideal for teatime.
Serve with hot toast or fresh bread and butter, with a salad,
or as a filling in sandwiches. When sealed with butter the potted foods
keep for up to 7 days in the refrigerator.

Flake the fish very finely and blend with half the butter and the rest of the ingredients. Pound or liquidize until smooth, but do not overwork the mixture. Put into 4 individual dishes and pour the remaining melted butter on top. Leave to cool completely before serving.

To Make a Change

Potted Herrings. Flaked cooked herrings, or kippers, or other full-flavoured fish may be used in the same way. Adjust the seasoning and spices as desired.

Potted Chicken and Ham. Follow the recipe above, using half cooked chicken and half cooked lean ham. Finely mince the meats then proceed as above. Other cooked meat or poultry may be used.

Potted Cheese. Use a mixture of grated or crumbled cheeses. Blend 8 oz/225 g (^{1}/2 lb) cheese with half the melted butter. Add 1-2 tablespoons (1^1/4-2^1/2 tbsp) port wine or dry sherry and 2-3 tablespoons chopped skinned fresh or pickled walnuts. Proceed as above.

The Modern Touch

Nutritionists will point out that traditional recipes for potted foods include a high percentage of butter. You can reduce this or blend polyunsaturated margarine with the fish or meat. Cover the food with foil instead of melted butter to keep the mixture moist.

Serves 4

8 oz/225 g (^{1}/2 lb) cooked salmon

4 oz/100 g (^{1}/2 cup) butter, melted

a pinch of grated or ground nutmeg

a pinch of ground mace

salt and pepper

2 teaspoons dry sherry or lemon juice

Index